Stopped in Our Tracks
Second Series

My teaching, if that is the word you want to use, has no copyright. You are free to reproduce, distribute, interpret, misinterpret, distort, garble, and do what you like; even claim authorship, without my consent or the permission of anybody.

U. G.

Stopped in Our Tracks
Second Series

(UG-Anecdotes, Comments and Reflections)

From the Notebooks of
K. CHANDRASEKHAR

MOTILAL BANARSIDASS INTERNATIONAL
DELHI

Delhi, 2025

© MOTILAL BANARSIDASS INTERNATIONAL
All Rights Reserved

ISBN : 978-81-969-8550-9 (PB)
ISBN : 978-81-969-8551-6 (HB)

Also available at :
MOTILAL BANARSIDASS INTERNATIONAL
41 U.A. Bungalow Road, (Back Lane) Jawahar Nagar, Delhi-110007
4261/3 (Basement), Ansari Road, Darya Ganj, New Delhi-110002
Shop#. 6, 241, Luz Ginza Complex, Luz Corner, Mylapore, Chennai - 600004
12/1A, 2nd Floor, Bankim Chatterjee Street, Kolkata - 700073
Stockist : Motilal Books, Ashok Rajpath, Near Kali Mandir, Patna-800004

No part of this book may be reproduced in any form or by any electronic or mechanical means including information storage and retrieval systems without permission in writing from the publishers, except by a reviewer who may quote brief passages in a review.

Printed in India by
MOTILAL BANARSIDASS INTERNATIONAL

Contents

Editor's Note	ix
Foreword by Mahesh Bhatt	xi

Part I

Truth is a moving target ...	1
"This is like a computer machine..."	8
On Education ...	16
Spiritual Experiences	20
With UG in Singapore....	29
"The body has no death..."	32
A Short Dialogue with UG	35
Some Interesting Things I Noticed in the Kathopanishad	42
UG and the Upanishads	50
Swami Poornanadagiri	53
Sarvepalli Radhakrishnan and UG	58

Part 2

"If you don't think...?"	62
"I am myself a thief..."	66
"You said no one will come this far...."	73
"No better medicine than spit to heal a wound..."	78
"Is it wrong to carry on in my tradition?"	80
Fifty per cent of the time ...	83
Satyanarayana's dream ...	84
Interpreting UG's horoscope	88
"UG is a Volcano ready to erupt...."	94

Non-existent Problem ...	97
Dr. Sudarshan ...	100
Facing Yama, the God of Death	102
Is Sadhana helpful?	106
Swami Vidyanarayana Tirtha	109
Knowledge needs separation ...	112

Part 3

"You have come to the wrong man"	117
The Story of Sharmila	123
"My photograph is more powerful than me..."	131
An Attempt to Strangle UG	134
"I met a man..."	136
A One-Night Stand	140
Bharati's New Year's Greetings	144
Mahesh: "Let my mother go…"	146
The Story of Shekhawat	150
The trouble the Delhi lady went through to meet UG ...	155
The Idiappam Story	157
The Way of UG's Health	160
Political Climate	162
Political Outrage	166
UG's Ways	169
"If you understand what I am saying at all, you wouldn't look at my face..."	171
Looking for Causes ...	173
"Release means total destruction..."	175

Part 4

A Burglary	180
The consciousness of "I" is implanted deeply	186
A Memento for the Barber	188
"What is your relationship to these things?"	190
"Why do you worry?"	194
"I know what happiness is not..."	197

"Do you think that there is any ultimate meaning, my son?"	198
Essential UG	200
Spirits and Satyanarayana	201
The Documentary Produced by BBC	205
Baba	209
"What do you want?"	211
My mind is agitated ...	213
"What can I do as an individual?..."	215
UG's words from What am I Saying?	217
Thinking that "I am..."	220
Path of Righteousness	223
Titbits from UG's Childhood	225
"You can never know that peace..."	227
Farm House Discussion	230
Valentine's Relatives	233
A Prayer to UG	237
In Conclusion . . .	240

Editor's Note

The wide interest in Chandrasekhar's first book, *Stopped in Our Tracks* prompted me to request him to select some more pieces for a second book. He complied with my request and sent me six of his notebooks from past years with selections for translation. I have arranged them in chronological order (starting from 1983). The reader should bear in mind, however, that some of the pieces may actually recall incidents from an earlier time or UG's earlier life.

In this book, you will find not only anecdotes about UG as Chandrasekhar witnessed them or heard about them (mostly from UG himself), but also Chandrasekhar's comments and reflections. These comments and reflections reveal Chandrasekhar's struggle to grasp and apply what UG says to his own life. We learn about his admiration for UG, his frustrations with him, his anger, remorse, his sadness and above all, his devotion towards and worship of UG. Chandrasekhar's struggles with UG's teachings would strike a familiar cord with anyone who has tried to understand UG. They are our struggles as well.

I thank Wendy Moorty for her diligent help in editing the text.

Narayana Moorty
Monterey, California
February 2007

Foreword

The minute I heard my first love story
I started looking for you, not knowing
How blind that was.
Lovers don't finally meet somewhere.
They are in each other all along.

— Rumi

Whether it is happy or unhappy, hopeful or devastating, the ending brings the story to what it itself is... the inevitable, the complete end.

On a quiet afternoon of March 14, 2007, in Vallecrosia, a quaint town in Italy, on the coast of the Mediterranean, Babu Chandrasekhar's guiding light and the love of his life, UG Krishnamurti, shouted out an order. "Leave now and get on with your life," said the light. "I want to die the way I lived... all alone, with no one looking over me."

Babu Chandrasekhar was devastated, but he also sensed that the end was near. Thus, he began the process of wrenching himself away from his own heartbeat. He prepared himself to break away from someone with whom he had spent more than three intense decades of his life, and who was not only the basis of his very existence but was also enshrined in his heart.

I still remember vividly what Babu did after hearing UG's command. He broke into Sanskrit shlokas, sat down at UG's feet. Then touching his feet, Babu prostrated his entire being before him as only a true devotee or a lover would do. When he got up he looked closely at UG as if he were absorbing him completely in that one long look. Then turning on his heel, Babu left the room where his master lived, never to return again.

As I led Babu out of the villa, where UG spent his last days, I can clearly recall the words I spoke to him. "This is death Babu, the end of your love story..." But little did I know that a love story like theirs never ends. I am not sure why, but whenever I think of the love story of Babu and UG I am reminded of Abu Bakr and Prophet Mohammed.

The story goes that when Abu Bakr saw the Prophet of God lying dead, he uncovered the mantle of the Yamani cloth that covered the Prophet's face and, kissing his forehead, said, "You are dearer than my father and mother. You have tasted the death which God had decreed, but oh Mohammed, a second death will never overtake you. You will never die again." And how right he was, because the emptiness which was created in the life of Abu Bakr with the passing away of his Master, could only be filled with the evangelistic fervour with which he went about spreading his word.

Stopped In Our Tracks, Series Two, originates from the same impulse. In this fascinating document, K Chandrasekhar has spun honey out of his encounters with UG. Whenever he was overwhelmed with UG's crazy wisdom or became shattered by his own sheer subversive behaviour, he documented it in a diary, which he has now generously made available to all of us. Indeed, this is a book to savour and read over and over again, because it is from the heart of a man who has bent low enough to hear the voice of his God.

Mahesh Bhatt
Mumbai
12-3-2010

Part I

Truth is a moving target...

May 16, 1983

It is impossible to define UG as "such and such" or to mould his teaching in a particular way or fit it within a certain frame. He is beyond our grasp. Right when you think you have a hold on him, he slips away with ease.

As soon as you think "O, I understand him now," there is another flash, another lightning or another manifestation quite contrary to what we think we have understood. "Contrary" does not in any way mean that he denies what he said earlier. Rather, the boundaries [*of our understanding*], the frontiers keep expanding as we listen to him, watch him and absorb what he says in our minds. Maybe that is the nature of truth!

"Truth is not something static. It's movement. Truth is a moving target," says UG.

That is the reason we cannot understand UG. I hesitate to write anything [*about him or his teaching*] because I fear that after all these years of trying to understand him, I have only gotten tired, and that whatever I say, think or write would only be an insult to him.

I remember reading sometime ago in the *Sivaparadha Stotram* of a devotee, who, while singing the praise of God, enumerates all his transgressions. He wails: "I committed many unpardonable crimes against you, such as, attributing a form to you whereas [*in reality*] you are formless, giving you a name whereas you are nameless, imagining you being in a specific place whereas you are omnipresent and worshipping you whereas you are merely a witness. How can you forgive me?"

My situation with regard to UG is similar. Once I look back, I feel that whatever I have written came just from my imagination.

Rabindranath [*Tagore*] in one of his poems asks himself, "What is the meaning of the songs in *Gitanjali*?" He answers briefly, "What do I know about their meaning? And who indeed knows their meaning?"

Nanduri [*Subba Rao*], who created an unimaginable empire of love, the vibrations of innocent and lovely hearts echoing in its poetic edifices, having given delicate form to two wonderful lovers, says philosophically, "When anyone asks 'Who is Enki?' I point to lights and shadows."

After I have written whatever I have to write and said whatever I have to say, I still feel like saying some more. Hence I add, "All these are thoughts that arose in my head after listening to UG and I wrote them down here. If you happen to read all this, please don't circumscribe what I have written here and say this is what UG is or what he says. He is an eternal riddle. If you find some answer to the riddle, the question will throw you into tangles and fly away."

How beautifully Dhurjati has written [in *Kalahastiswara Sataka*]:

If truth were to be described
Can poetry contain it?
Shame on poets like me
Oh! Lord of Sri Kalahasti!

I don't even have the confidence which Potana shows when he

says, "I shall clarify what I have seen, heard and learned from the wise ones..."

* * *

"I wish I could give you a feel of this..."

August 1, 1983

"I wish I could give you a feel of this. Then you would never be interested in it. You wouldn't touch it with a ten-foot pole," UG says. You can't presume that these words are an exaggeration. Perhaps they are true. How could there be any experience when everything we have imagined about that state is turned upside down; when the mind itself disappears along with the image it has built; when our whole existence fizzles out like fog; when the endless flow of our experience comes to a grinding halt; when whatever we thought was unmoving, starts trampling around; and when the snow peak of a mountain we approached admiring its beauty, all of a sudden cracks down creating tremors in the earth and sky and flows as a stream? Who can experience it? When everything burns in that stream like firewood; when the notions of "I" and "mine" rise like sparks in the fire of time for a little while and merge back into that fire; when the inhaled and exhaled breath kindles that fire like air in the bellows, making its flames much brighter; when the series of electrical energy waves radiate with lightning speed vibrating each and every nerve – who can imagine such a state? Who can wish for such a state? Is it some indescribable bliss? Is it a group of waves in a limitless ocean of peace? Oh my child, what are you thinking? What are you imagining? Are you still dreaming lying on your bed? When the experience burns away like fuel in fire because there is no one who can recognise it as bliss, who remains to describe that experience, to relish it? Who is there that thinks that he cannot bear the heat of the flames of that fire? It wouldn't leave you even if you don't want it. It won't calm down until it reduces everything to ashes like a wildfire.

* * *

Fixing one's mind in meditation...

August 2, 1983

My mind has been disappointed because it could not stay in meditation. In the past, I used to lament the whole day saying, "Alas, I couldn't fix my mind. I have lost the grace of God." On the other hand, on days when my mind was able to meditate steadily, I would experience great peace and simple joy. No matter what I was witnessing, eating or doing, I would be in some transcendental state, as if I were watching things from behind glass mirrors. Then I would strive to repeat that state and enhance it. However, with this endeavour my torture started. I could not meditate and I could not quit. What a great help UG was for me when he came into my life. The first thing he did was to get me away from such immature perceptions.

"Such amazing experiences are natural. They come and they go. You should remain as if you haven't noticed them. If you give them any importance, then they make you feel like wanting them again," UG would say.

"Those who take drugs like LSD have even greater experiences. Some have strange experiences – they witness many wonderful scenes, visions and *mandalas* [mystical designs]. Those are all the effects of the chemical changes that occur in their brains. More than that, there is nothing spiritual about them. But because of those experiences, they fall into the illusion that they are achieving something spiritual and they try to delve deeper into spiritual practice.

"As a matter of fact, in that state you will not be anyone and will not experience anything. You wouldn't know whether you have thoughts or not, or what you are experiencing or whether you are experiencing sorrow or bliss.

"Ultimately, even the experience of God is a worthless experience within the limitless consciousness. No matter how great the experience is, there is a contamination in that consciousness.

"Isn't it foolish to strive to experience it while saying at the same time that it is unreachable by mind or speech and that it is beyond experience?" UG would explain in this manner.

"Then what must I do now?", when I asked UG this question three years ago in Goa, he said, "You don't need to do anything. Those who practice are not really in any higher state than you."

Just do nothing. I think it is said quite well in the Gita that, "*atma-samstham manah krtva na kincid api cintayet* [the mind should be fixed on the self alone and should think of nothing else]." Dedicate everything to the Lord of All in your heart; and surrender all your thoughts to Him, always think, "I am not concerned. I don't exist; only you are everything" – [it doesn't matter] if you have thoughts or don't have any, if you are happy or are not, whether you are able to fix your mind in meditation or not. Who am I in the first place that I should do something?

If there is any practice that we can do, only the following seems possible:

Yato-yato niscarati manascancalam asthiram
Tatastat -niyamyai tad Atmanyeva vasam nayet

[Whenever the unsteady and fickle mind wanders off somewhere, one should bring it back by practising restraint and then controlling it.]

For the little while you sit, whenever your mind or thoughts wander off, you must bring them back to yourself and dedicate them to the Lord of All. That's all I can do now.

The mind must come into meditation naturally. It's not a practice. Does the *Gayatri* meditation happen due to my effort? The *japa* indeed starts as though some force unknown to me pushes itself forward. When I remain alone, even when I am meditating, some thoughts do indeed go on.

Malato karame phire jib phiremukhamahim
Manavato dasadasi phire yahto sumiran nahi

says Kabir, [Rosary keeps rotating in the hands/so does the tongue in the mouth (doing *japa*)/but the mind keeps wandering off in all the directions. /Surely, this is no meditation!] It's literally true. Still there is no other choice. It's not in my hands. I don't know when it [*Gayathri japa*] will stop.

* * *

UG's Appearance

Once as I sat looking at UG's photograph, I wondered why his hair was so long. Although UG does not let his hair grow quite as long as actors in the drama companies do, his hair grows down to his neck. "My ears are big. The hair is helpful in hiding them," he says when someone asks him about his hairstyle. I don't know if anyone went on to ask him, "Why should you hide your ears? Why can't they be seen?"

I think in the *Science of the Bodily Signs*, they had examined the characteristics of the organs of holy men. They concluded that great teachers and seers journeying on the spiritual path have large ears. You will understand that, if you see the paintings or sculptures of Gautama the Buddha. "Dad" Chalam also had big ears. So did Shau [*Sowris, Chalam's daughter, a mystic*]. I think that Bhagavan had large ears, too.

In the photographs taken before the Calamity, UG's hair looks normal. I have two photographs in my album, passport photos – one three years before the Calamity and the other three years after it. It's strange that there is no resemblance between the two pictures. It's hard to tell that the two pictures are of the same person. I don't understand how there is such a change even in the face. It's unimaginable that an adult, who has not even passed his middle age, could still change so much in a span of just six years.

Once I was leafing through the Ayurvedic manual *Charaka Samhita* in the World Culture Institute Library, and I noticed a mention of how the characteristics of a penis can differ from person to person. According to the manual, the penises of *Jnanis* and yogis are soft like jelly. Later, when Swami Sundarananda explained about the Indrajit *Asana* and showed me its photograph, I thought that Charaka's statements were accurate. "Sex is impossible for a person in this state," says UG. Maybe that's true. "Not that he becomes impotent or any such thing. Even an erection may be possible. But there is no build up, without which sex cannot be achieved," he adds.

* * *

Brahmacharya

That is why UG maintains that the ancient sages who lived with their families were not real seers. He asserts that they are the cause of our present [*deplorable*] state. It is not clear why the term *brahmacharya* came to acquire the meaning of being free from sexual pleasures. If you look at the meaning of the word in Sanskrit, it means "moving in Brahman" or "being devoted to Brahman" or some such thing. There is no reference to sexual copulation. Today, however, people give quite contrary interpretations to the word *brahmachari*, namely, "he who doesn't indulge in sexual pleasures" or "an unmarried person." Perhaps they noticed that those devoted to Brahman have no sexual desires and so they fell into the misconception that *brahmacharya* means the absence of sexual desires.

Be that as it may, it's indisputable that in that "non-dual" state there is a total absence of bodily concern and craving for sensual enjoyment. There is no such thing as arriving at that state.

"This is not a thing to be attained. It is not a state which you enter at one time and come out at another. It's always there... there is no such thing as a "fall" from that state..."

The state of a *yoga bhrashtha* [*one who has fallen from yoga*] is nothing but a bizarre and abnormal aberration before reaching that state.

* * *

"This is like a computer machine..."

August 5, 1983

When Arjuna asks:

*sthita-prajñasya kā bhāṣā
samādhi-sthasya keśava
sthita-dhīḥ kim prabhāṣeta
kim āsīta vrajeta kim*

[What are the characteristics of the one who is established in wisdom and absorbed in *samadhi*, Krishna? How does a person of steady wisdom speak and what is his language? How does he sit and how does he walk?]

Krishna does not answer Arjuna's question directly, rather he enumerates the characteristics of an enlightened man and describes his state. Perhaps Arjuna wonders how a man devoted to Brahman conducts his affairs in the world. How can a man who always stays in *samadhi* carry on his practical life?

How can a yogi, who sports in a state devoid of volition, be capable of performing the duties that he has to carry on?

prajahati yada kaman
sarvan partha mano-gatan
atmany evatmana tustah
sthita-prajnas tadocyate

[When a person renounces all the desires that arise in the mind, Partha, and finds contentment within his self, then he is said to be established in wisdom.]

"How can such a man carry on his worldly affairs?" was Arjuna's next question. The mind and the desires arising from it are indeed the basis and primary motivation for activities. Krishna himself admits this at some place:

Nahi kascit ksanamapi jatu tisthatyakarmakrt

[No one can live even for a moment without action.]

The promptings are so powerful. Then, in the yogi who lacks them, what are the motivational springs which prompt him to act?

That's where the complication lies. The mind which attributes cause-effect relationship to every action cannot imagine that actions are possible without any cause or prompting. This truth is beyond the human intellect. Because its nature is not to admit to anything that it cannot understand, the mind feels stifled by its own questions.

When UG states "This is like a machine, a computer machine," we begin to understand it to some degree.

However, in this human machine, the thing called "I" is implanted in each organ. This notion of "I" is carried away in the constantly flowing flux of experience with great speed into a beginning-less and endless void. There is no room even to take a short breath. "Who am I?" is not the correct question. It presupposes that "I exist." The ideal question is, "What is this 'I'?" said UG once.

It's the same with any question. No matter how much one

struggles and wails, there is no clear way. There is no release from this chaotic network of darkness and delusion.

"Dad" Chalam kept beating his wings, trying for release till the end of his life. I haven't met another person who thought more deeply, more straightforwardly and more profoundly than Chalam. I cannot find in any another person the qualities of honesty, broadmindedness, generosity and truth-seeking that I have seen in Chalam. Since UG lies beyond all these perceptions, even though he is similar to Chalam in many respects, yet Chalam cannot be compared to UG.

The same characteristics of fearlessness, steadfastness and purity that Chalam strove to acquire all his life, were inherently inculcated in UG and established him as a unique person. But it is, indeed, a mistake to call UG a "person". You can call someone a person only when he has personality. How can there be a certain "personality" when the "person" has broken loose from its shell and the bird has flown into the sky and the ripples on the water have spread beyond the boundaries set by the mind to become dissolved in a state transcending the mind? "Dad", who has been there only till recently, is no longer there! But isn't he within me, merged in my innermost core, in my thoughts and in my breath?

* * *

"Nothing will remain at the end..."

August 30, 1983

Days, months and years are rolling away. What I wanted to accomplish still remains. I can't quite think clearly *what* I want to accomplish. There have been many times when I thought to myself, "Not this, there is something else. My life cannot be spent in just earning a living." But what should I do otherwise? Meditation? Social service? Writing? What do I want to do? I am not too keen on any of these things. If I had been keen on any of these, there have been ample opportunities in my life to pursue one or the other of these. What remains now is stewing in the feeling that my life is all being wasted away in idleness.

"There is nothing besides this. Only because you are deluded in thinking that there is something else, you get such feelings," says UG. True. That sounds plausible. Then I must think "there is nothing else." But I shudder at the very idea of thinking from that point of view. Eight years ago, Vajir asked UG, "What will remain after death?" "Nothing will," said UG repeatedly and emphatically. How agitated Vajir looked! There was trembling in his voice. Later that day, he said to me, "UG says so honestly that nothing will remain. Think about it. What else is there? What is the meaning of this life?" while looking at me sadly. He never saw UG again. "No need to," he said. How deeply and intensely did that conversation and that day he spent with UG impact his life! In January that year, Vajir published *Sahasi*, his poetic compilation. He poured all of UG's teaching into his first poem, "Nothing will remain at the end." He died believing the same! Vajir, where are you, my friend? Are you really there? Are you searching for what remains? You would surely let me know if you find anything, won't you? Is this all, finally? Is this all? Will nothing remain? How horrible! What is all this turmoil for, then?

* * *

Asanas

This morning when I was doing the *Savasana* after my usual "Salutations to the Sun", I was reminded of UG's words: "Yoga must start with *Savasana*. Sometime after the movement of *prana* ceases and the body becomes rigid like a stick, it then becomes awake again. Before it comes back to the normal state, it makes spontaneous movements and increases the blood circulation to the nerves. Those "gentlemen" who observed those movements popularised them by defining them as means of spiritual practice and teaching them. That's how the present thinking that yoga is nothing but *asanas* has come into being," he said.

One day, UG showed us at our home how to do the *Savasana*. You should lie down on your back entwining the big toes of both feet with each other, interlocking the fingers of both hands and turning the hands inside, folding them and placing them on your chest. When you lie down like that on your back, the static currents inside the body circulate around the body in a circular fashion without being discharged. This is a new theory. He explained it in a very practical fashion. I tried to do it by lying down as he had instructed. I could only experience that the body was in a state of tension; I didn't experience the feeling of relief one normally does in *Savasana*. I must ask UG once again and learn this procedure of *Savasana* more clearly.

Thirteen years ago, UG used to perform *asanas* early in the morning. I would also do my *asanas* at that time. One day, while I was doing the *asanas*, UG came and stood in front of me and corrected some of my *asanas* while I was doing them. "They run counter to the natural movements of the body. When I realised this, I stopped doing *asanas*," says UG.

There is a need for a lot of research into these matters where UG has shed new light.

* * *

Walking around naked...

Avadhuta Sadasiva Brahmendra apparently always went around naked. It seems that the devotee of Kali, Sri Ramakrishna Paramahamsa, whether he was in *samadhi* or out of it, used to be unmindful of whether his clothing was intact or not. The resident of Arunagiri, Ramana Bhagavan, escaped the bother of clothes by wearing a loin cloth. Did all these people behave like that in order to show their spiritual superiority and their lack of concern for the body? True to the adage, "The one who wears a loin cloth is indeed a fortunate man," did they find happiness in renouncing everything?

UG gives a scientific explanation for these people's fondness for being naked. It seems that intense electricity is generated as a result of the chemical changes that have taken place in their bodies. Great heat is experienced in the body and unexplained outbursts of energy become routine. Clothing is an obstacle for the circulation of that energy. Synthetic fabrics like terelene or nylon make the problem even worse. That's why UG never uses them. He always wears cotton or silk clothes in this country. That must be why people who observed *madi* [ritually clean clothing] always wore silk clothes. People compete with each other to give the finest silk clothes to UG. Although he feels irked, UG accepts the clothes out of compassion that if he does not take them, the feelings of those who would like to give would be hurt. At times when he is in his room alone, he removes all his clothing because he can't stand the heat in his body.

* * *

"What does UG say?"

April 1, 1986

Two nights ago, when I went into the hall, it was filled with people: Shanta's friend Pushpa, Pushpa's husband and the other friends who are usually there. I sat in a corner, next to the stairs that go up to the second floor. Pushpa's husband seemed to be in middle age and apparently, had a job in the Indian Institute of Science. Subbanna, as usual, sat leaning against the wall, with stretched legs, dozing off.

"Come, Valentine, come and sit in this chair," UG said and showed her the chair. She climbed down three steps slowly and sat in the chair.

"Chandrasekhar, suppose somebody asks you 'What does UG say?' how would you answer in brief?" asked UG suddenly.

That's a question which UG routinely asks. He is curious to hear how one elaborates on it. As I couldn't think of anything, I didn't answer. UG repeated his question; so I attempted a reply:

"Everyone is seeking something or the other, as he is not satisfied with what he is. You point out through your discussions or conversations the futility of this search and you knock out all the goals created by the society and culture … You explain that anything that is experienced, however profound the nature of that experience may be, is worthless, because it is born out of the knowledge one already has about it. There is no such thing as a new experience at all. Knowledge creates the experience, which further strengthens the knowledge, which is a vicious circle. You show that one is helpless in a given situation, but one doesn't want to accept that situation. We constantly want to do something with that which is creating misery and conflict," I tried to summarise thus, but UG appeared unimpressed.

"Why do you all come here day after day? Why? I don't offer you anything! I haven't invited any of you. So why do you come? Haven't some of you been coming for 15 or 16 years? Why? What do you want?" UG was hammering the assembly with his questions.

Yes, this question intrigues me, too. Why do they come? Why do I go to UG? What do I want from him?

"There's a lot of entertainment here. Why not leave it at that?" Venkatramayya said laughingly.

"What entertainment? I have no objection, but there are better entertainments elsewhere. Why come here? Why are you interested in this kind of a thing?" asked UG.

In the meantime, the Australians came up with their usual air of extreme reverence towards UG and settled down on the floor.

UG noticed a plastic bag in their hands. "I think you should stop bringing all these things to us," UG admonished. Max giggled.

"May I ask you one thing?" said UG. "Why do you come here day after day? Why? What do you want?"

Max was speechless for sometime. Perhaps they were not prepared for such a question that would hit them directly.

"You are like a magnet UG! You draw us all to you irresistibly," said Max with folded hands.

"No, I don't think so. I really want to understand why you all come here. Please don't get me wrong. If nobody is here it's just fine with me. It's not a motiveless thing. When you come and throw questions at me, you are creating a motive in me. Otherwise, I just sit here – I can sit and talk for 24 hours. It never exhausts me. But this talking is not a self-fulfilling thing to me. Obviously you want something. You imagine that I am some kind of god-knows-what. But actually and factually, you have no way of knowing anything about me, and much less about yourself. You project your ideas on me and hope to get something. Basically you are interested in changing yourself. But my question is, why that change should be only in the future – tomorrow - but not today, right here and now? Why? You hope to be something, whatever you want to be, only tomorrow. So, it is the hope that keeps you going."

Suddenly Mr. Sivaraman, the lawyer, butted in and said, "According to law, once we make a contract we are always bound by that. There is no way of breaking the contract. That is why we all are here." Everybody in the assembly burst into laughter, including UG.

* * *

On Education...

April 5, 1986 (Saturday)

Mahesh is expected tomorrow morning. Dinesh is also coming from Goa. Last night, UG was reading out a few excerpts from the manuscript prepared by Mahesh – the article to be published in the *Illustrated Weekly* next month – "UG and JK". Mahesh has a writing style of his own, which is indeed fascinating.

Tonight there were not many in the hall. About 8 p.m., Mr. Harish Singh of Ooty suddenly showed up with a person in an ochre robe whom he introduced to UG as his elder brother. Harish is a teacher in the Blue Mountain School in Ooty. He had worked earlier in the Rishi Valley School of JK and, after meeting UG in Bombay three years ago, left it.

"We've arrived just now, at 7 p.m., on our way to Madras. My brother wanted to see you and I thought we could spend a couple of hours with you," said Harish to UG.

The brother was evidently a follower of Rajneesh; he was stroking the mala on his neck with his fingers.

"When are you going to Madras?" UG asked Harish.

"This very night. Tomorrow, I'll put my brother on the train to Calcutta and I'll go back to Ooty. I'm planning to come again to Bangalore at the end of this month or early next month."

"We're moving into a new house soon, a bigger place," UG told him.

Harish looked surprised. "This month? Is the place far off? How can I find it when I come next?"

"It's not very far. Just ten minutes by walk from here. If you come back here, you can get the directions from someone here. That's no problem."

"So, UG, you're going to have a bigger place. Are you also planning to have a secretary, intermediaries and all that, too?" Harish was trying to have a dig.

"Why? Do you want to apply for his secretary's job?" I countered Harish on UG's behalf.

Harish smiled. "I may not mind being his secretary, but I don't think we two would get on well," he said.

UG nodded and said, "That's true, especially not after all that you wrote on education in that *Blue Print*. [*UG was referring to the editorial written by Harish in their in-house magazine, a copy of which he had sent to UG earlier.*] How can you write all that? 'Education is the only panacea for all the evils that the society is a prey to…' – you wrote something to that effect."

"Why not, UG?" recoiled Harish, "You feel that way, because you are not an educationalist. What's wrong with my statement?"

"Why do you want to use poor children for your own self-aggrandisement? They don't need all that. I don't think environment plays any role in shaping the individual," UG remarked. "Now they say we're all genetically controlled. Two students go to the same school, to the same teacher and receive the same kind of instruction, but each comes out differently. How do you explain that?"

He said further, "Now it has become a fashion to start new schools. With all these spiritual and religious organisations, Ramakrishna Mission, even Chinmayananda – everyone is bent on educating the children in his or her particular school of thinking. Why brainwash poor helpless children? What's so marvellous about your particular method of schooling? How is it distinct and different from the regular schools?"

Harish moved uneasily on the carpet. "It's distinct and different in the sense that we don't force and punish the children. We try to create an [*open*] atmosphere."

"That's all the more wrong. 'Spare the rod and spoil the child.' What's wrong in punishing? When I was a boy, I was hit with a pencil on my finger by my teacher and was given "imposition" because I spelled the word "February" wrong – I had to write that word in the sand twenty times. Of course, I had no courage to hit my teacher back. I attended very ordinary schools. What's wrong with me? There's cut-throat competition everywhere; yet you teach the children not to compete. The atmosphere you're trying to create is false. It doesn't exist. You're only making them misfits in the world."

"But I earn my bread working there…"

"That's all right; that's acceptable to me. You may very well work there and earn more. There are people in this world with more money than sense. It's a status symbol to send their children to private schools, spending thousands. That's all right. But I'm questioning the usefulness of such schools. What's the result? Show me one individual – a leader – who is a perfect product of these schools?"

"Krishnamurti and I had the same argument. He wanted me to go and teach in Rishi Valley School and admit my children there. I told him, 'That's the last thing I will ever do. What's so marvellous about your school? Why force those children to wear uniforms and watch sunsets from a hilltop?' *Astachal* they call the hill. You force your ideas on them. Actually, they live in their own world. I think it was Newman who said, 'Universities polish pebbles and dim diamonds.'"

Suddenly UG remembered something. "Is it true that in the Rajghat School, students are beating their teachers?"

"Yes, it's very much true," said Harish, nodding his head.

"That must have shattered the Old Man," said UG referring to JK.

* * *

UG was narrating about his earlier days in Banaras.

"Every year I used to spend three months in Banaras – for seven years in a row. I was giving lectures. I learned more from my grandmother about Vedanta than from my professor. Even the fakirs on the banks of Ganges in Banaras taught me more.

"I was a National Lecturer of the Theosophical Society. I used to visit North India, keeping my headquarters in Banaras."

"Did you pick up some Hindi while you were there?"

"Hindi?" UG laughed and exclaimed, "Down with Hindi! Down with North Indian music, too. I don't like them. My Hindi stopped with the *Pahli*, *Dusri* and *Tisri* standard books."

* * *

Spiritual Experiences

"You must have had many experiences–spiritual experiences in those days."

"Oh, yes, all kinds of experiences – *samadhi* states, you name it. But I soon realised that there is nothing to all those experiences."

"You once said you had a great mystical experience after listening to Krishnamurti. Was it after you said goodbye to him in Bombay?"

"No, it was much earlier, when I was attending his talks in Madras at Vasanta Vihar. I had a death experience."

"You said that you could have easily started a huge organisation drawing from the strength of that experience."

"Yes, that's true. In Madras, around 1953, I asked Krishnamurti the question, 'What kick do you get, sir, from all these discourses?' Later, Krishnamurti, during one of his talks, suddenly asked, 'What do you have to say, sir?' pointing towards me. I thought he was asking the man sitting in front of me. However, when that man stood up to speak, Krishnamurti said, 'Not you sir, the young man sitting behind you.' From then on, we were both involved in heated discussions. Krishnamurti never allowed others to interfere with us. 'No, sir, we have to thrash out the whole thing,' he would say. One day, he was talking about the subconscious, unconscious and stuff like that. I asked him, 'I don't see any subconscious in me. Why are you talking about the subconscious?' He said, 'Sir, for you and me, there is no such thing as the subconscious. But I am talking to these people about that.' Then I thought, 'You are using me as a sounding board to reach these people. Then I am not interested in this game. I'm off,' and stopped discussing with him. During those days we were mostly discussing death and the death experience. One day, I suddenly felt that I was dying."

"Was that while listening to Krishnamurti?"

"Yes, it was right in the hall. In those days, he had smaller gatherings of 100 or 150 people. I felt that something like a vacuum pump was sucking the life out of me. I felt a terrible fear of dying."

"Did you tell Krishnamurti about that experience?"

"Yes. I talked to him about it at great length. He listened to me patiently for half-an-hour. At the end, he said, 'If there is anything to that, sir, it will certainly express itself in its own way. Otherwise, it will fade out.' It did fade out after some time."

"How did you get to feel that you could start a huge organisation on the strength of that experience?"

"You see, I was able to see Krishnamurti's teaching with more clarity in the light of that experience. But I had to fall back on him for that clarity. That dependence created a revolt in me. Finally, I stopped going to his talks."

* * *

Powers

"You were saying that you had acquired some powers as a result of that experience. What were those powers?"

"Yes, I had all those powers. By looking at a person I could tell his past, present and future. Sometimes, I did tell people what I saw. But soon I realised that telling them about their future created more trouble for them."

"Do you remember any such instance?"

"Once, Mr. Olivetti, an Italian business magnate, came to me. When I looked at him, I told him he had cancer. He was startled. His doctors had just recently assured him, after several tests, that he did not have cancer. But my observation created a doubt in him. He rushed to his doctors and they confirmed that he had cancer. He died of it soon after."

"But such flashes are not uncommon, at least to a few."

"This is nothing marvellous – that's what I maintain. There is no power outside of man and there is nothing about supernatural powers here. Everybody has them. Sometimes they work and sometimes they don't – it works in fifty per cent cases. After the Calamity or whatever had happened to me, the first thing I said to Valentine was 'I have lost all my powers.'"

"How did you know that you had lost them?"

"...because nothing was coming to my head. Now I know that whatever comes in here [*pointing to his head*] must be true. It cannot be false. But I have no use of those thoughts. There is nobody to translate them. So, they get burnt there. That's the energy, sir, not the frictional energy created by thought.

"Here, this is like a drum – a perfectly tuned instrument. You come here and play it. The lyric is yours, the tune is yours and the beat is yours. The drum has nothing to do with what melodies you produce. It's not interested," said UG, referring to himself.

* * *

"Here and now..."

"'Here and now' has no meaning. "Here" is space and "now"

is time. Thought creates the space and the time because thought is space and thought is time. So, nothing can happen in the "here and now". Anything that is captured and projected by thought is worthless. How can thought, which is born in space and time, end itself in space and time?

"It's always tomorrow. When tomorrow arrives, it [*thought*] pushes it further. So, nothing can happen here and now – "the eternal present". All that is nonsense.

"What is there to happen? There's nothing to happen."

* * *

"The goal creates its opposite..."

"The root cause of corruption lies in the religious thinking of man. Religion is responsible for the corruption, crime and selfishness that we see around us. It's the goal that creates its opposite. As long as there is love, so long will there be hate. It's love that creates hate; it's selflessness that creates selfishness. When the goal [*to be selfless*] goes, with that selfishness also goes. But you don't seem to understand that the goal is not different from you; you *are* the goal. You *are* the selfishness. It's not in your interest to end yourself. So, the logical structure evolves more logic around this argument and continues. Otherwise, it collapses."

* * *

Peace of Mind

"There is no such thing as peace of mind. As long as you think you have what you call "mind", so long will you be restless. Restlessness is the nature of the mind.

"Peace of mind will blow your mind! You can't ask for it, because... How can you ask for something whose nature you have no idea about?

"Your wanting to be "peaceful" is creating the restlessness. Otherwise, there is perfect peace in that organism. There is no need to do anything. The body is very peaceful.

"What they are offering in the marketplace are just the pain-killers. There is no such thing as a cure anywhere. If you want those temporary pain-killers, you can jolly well go to those [*who sell them*] in the marketplace. Don't come here and ask for "peace of mind". Whatever peace of mind is left there, will also be lost!"

* * *

"First you master the art of sleeping while standing..."

April 19, 1991

Sleep–a deep sleep and the state of being awake have always interested Vedantam Satyanarayana. He somehow managed to bring those subjects into his conversation with UG this evening. We were all sitting on the terrace trying to avoid the sweltering heat in the glass room. As soon as I returned from my work, Frank began describing the harrowing experience of jealousy that was burning inside him. UG kept the flame burning purposely by his "educated guesses" about Frank's sordid state of affairs.

"The Observer video tape has arrived at last!" said UG as we were sitting on the mats. The courier who had brought it had trouble locating our house because he was told that the house number was 10 instead of the correct number 40. Vedantam Satyanarayana gave the courier the wrong number. "He is so much preoccupied with Ultimate Reality that he never noticed the number of the house painted in large figures on the gate," someone said.

Radhakishan remarked, "Sir, how can you know Brahman when you don't know the number of the house which you visit every day, both morning and evening?" We all laughed.

The subject of sleep kept even the sleeping Subbanna awake. "First, how do you know that you are awake?" asked UG. "You have been told that... it's only knowledge."

"I don't accept that knowledge is coming in between the sensory perceptions..." asserted Vedantam.

At last, UG said, "Look at the tree. Why do you say it's green?"

"Because it is green."

"It's not because it is green. You really don't know what it is. You've been taught that it is green. That is knowledge. In exactly the same way, you know that you are awake, asleep or dreaming. There is no such thing as reality. I don't know whether I'm awake or asleep."

Subbanna become more interested in the talk of sleep. He told us he was practising sleeping while standing in the city bus.

He wanted UG to teach him how to sleep with his eyes wide open. "First you master the art of sleeping while standing; then we'll see about the other way of sleeping," replied UG.

"If the great heritage of your country has produced people like you, then I don't see any reason to feel proud about this culture." This was the last line in the nine-and-a-half minute video we watched of the dialogue between UG and Mahesh, which will be marketed by the *Observer* in New Delhi. Who were the others interviewed in the tape? Maybe L. K. Advani, Rajiv Gandhi and such other personalities.

"So you come between two politicians [*in the video*]?" quipped Vedantam Satyanarayana.

"That's better. JK's talks were shown in the United States between two hardcore sex shows. Otherwise, who would be interested?"

* * *

Energy Movements...

August 25, 1991, Sunday

It was the afternoon, around 4:30 p.m. I suddenly felt an urge to meet Vedam Satyanarayana. I wasn't sure whether he would be home; so I first telephoned him. He answered the phone and said he was not well. He had been seriously ill for quite some time during the past month – he contracted typhoid and had been recovering slowly. I decided that Suguna and I must go and see him; and in spite of the overcast sky which was threatening to rain, we reached his house by 5:30 p.m.

He looked very weak and obviously had lost a lot of weight. He said he was on leave till the end of this month. Then he started talking about many matters including money and Suguna's health.

I want to record here his account of a dream he had had while he was ill. When he had high fever and his body was dehydrated, he noticed peculiar feelings of energy movements. Satyanarayana feels that this was not a hallucination.

"I suddenly felt an electrical current passing through my ankles and bursting through my hips. It all happened so suddenly that I don't know what exactly had happened. It took place a couple of times and then suddenly the electrical discharge started in my head, and like a wave filled my entire body and got discharged through my penis. Again, it lasted only a fraction of a second and the discharge left a feeling of irritation at the tip of my penis. There was no semen or fluid but just this sudden discharge of electrical energy with great force. It was so severe that the irritation lasted till the next morning.

"Then some sort of fear gripped me every time I lay down. The energy would start with wave-like movements. Then I would get up and the movements would stop. I tried to sit up the whole night, knowing that the energy would hit me again if I lay down. During that time I had a vivid dream: UG was lying flat on a cot with closed eyes. I was gripped with the fear of death while I looked at him. He spread both his palms open and I understood that he wanted my palms to be placed on them. When I did that, he clasped them tight.

I thought he was going to transmit some of his energy. Suddenly he started mumbling something to himself. I thought he was saying some prayers and I was curious to know what he was murmuring. When I listened closely, to my utter astonishment, I heard his usual pet lines, which he often repeats during his talks. Immediately, I recalled in the dream that Sri Aurobindo used to advise his followers to read his words or some passages at random from his books. He believed that just those sounds have a tremendous effect on the human body.

"After that, the dream ended and I suddenly felt very ecstatic and then became normal again."

This shows how UG's words and deeds, which are charged with great power, can help certain people. Satyanarayana, having felt that he was on the brink of death, suddenly regained his vitality after this dream.

"Peanuts activate sex glands..."

Major is experimenting with natural foods. He now survives on sprouted legumes, fruits and so on. "If you eat banana peels, the chemical substance in them is said to give some 'kick'; and if you eat bananas you will go 'bananas'," comments UG. "Don't eat peanuts. They are supposed to activate the sex glands. That's what they have found after experimenting with peanut butter."

Major's new problem seems to be that he gets aggravated. UG, on his part, has strong opinions about "natural" diet. He never misses a chance to take a dig at those who religiously pursue dietary discipline for their spiritual goals. "You can gobble up the newborn baby next door to you and still be spiritual," is more his line of thinking. UG's food habits hardly fit into any natural diet regimen, yet he is seventy-four years old. "I take a pint of cream every day and what's wrong with me? I have no cholesterol problem. Shoot at sight and on sight all those bastards who talk of natural diet!" UG responds. For seventy-four years he has maintained good health.

* * *

"Being reborn as a cockroach is better..."

Vedantam Satyanarayana enters the garden looking well-fed and chewing betel leaves. UG makes room for him next to him on the swing, "Come, sir, sit here."

Satyanarayana half-seriously and half-jokingly enquires, "What's the current status of enlightenment, sir?"

"Same as yesterday; and it's going to be the same tomorrow too," replies UG without a moment's pause. Everyone laughs. UG asks Satyanarayana, "Sir, what will you do with enlightenment, assuming for a moment that you do get it? What will you do?"

"The trouble is that you want to know you are in your natural state. There is no knowing," UG adds.

"If we don't attain enlightenment, who knows, we may have to be born again as a cat or a dog..." Satyanarayana replies.

"That's better," said UG, "a cockroach is even better. You will survive the nuclear holocaust. How old are you, sir?"

"Sixty-seven," said Satyanarayana.

"You're a kid as compared to me. I am seventy-four," UG said mockingly.

* * *

With UG in Singapore...

i. "Poor Indian..."

Events from February 8, 1992.

This year, UG has asked Suguna and me to travel with him to Singapore via Hong Kong. On this day the two of us (Suguna and I) walked around the streets of Singapore and were very tired. All of us had walked around a shopping mall called Dynasty on Orchard Street and around many other shopping malls. Finally, wanting to head back to the hotel, we hailed a taxi. The taxi driver asked us where we wanted to go. When we mentioned our destination, his facial expressed changed. "You can walk there in five minutes. You call a taxi for that?" he asked us mockingly. "What do you have to lose? We've been walking around for five hours and are tired. Let's go," we said and collapsed into the taxi, all four of us (including Julie). While driving the taxi, that Chinese man looked at UG and asked his age. He continued, "My father is older than you and walks for miles and miles every day. The ladies in Singapore are lazy. They are too lazy to walk." "We are just poor Indians visiting here," UG said. When he heard 'poor Indians', the cab driver turned around, squinted his eyes and said, "What, you think you are poor Indians after flying here in an airplane for such a distance and staying in an expensive hotel to have fun? I can't even afford to own a car. No matter how many years

I work, I can never take a vacation. If I don't work I don't eat. What about people like me?" the Chinese man retorted. He said driving one's own car or owning a taxi is a complicated affair in Singapore. "There are car companies. I rent a taxi from one of them and drive it. This taxi is not my own," he said. When UG repeatedly went on about "poor Indians", he said angrily, "I don't want to hear that word. You talk about being poor but actually you are rich." "I'll take you through a shortcut to the hotel nearby. Don't call a taxi the next time you go for such a short distance," he advised, stopping near the hotel. When UG placed an ample reward in his hands for his generosity and advice, his face showed that he was mighty pleased.

* * *

ii. Singapore Chat

Another incident from Singapore: I wrote about a taxi driver before. Now this was another one. He was a Tamil Muslim and his name was Ismail. When he spoke in Tamil, UG became tremendously affectionate towards him. To add to it, when he learned that he was a Muslim, he grew even fonder of him. After sitting in the taxi, he asked him, "Do you know where Hotel Metropole is?" in Tamil. The driver replied with a serious face, "You shouldn't ask a Singapore driver if he knows where a certain place is. You should just tell him to go there," trying to teach us a lesson. Then he talked like a chatterbox for the length of time he drove the taxi. He poured abuse on Bangarappa, the Chief Minister of Karnataka. He cursed the Tamils from Sri Lanka for not speaking in their mother tongue. He praised UG to the skies for speaking good Tamil. "How long have you lived here?" UG asked him. Apparently, he had come in 1953. And he was quite happy here. Still, he wanted to go back to India. "No matter how long you live here, this is a foreign country. It's comfortable here. But living in our country is different from making a living here," said the taxi driver with feeling.

* * *

iii. The movie star Sridevi with UG...

That day it was February 10, 1992. It was rather cold in Hong

Kong. There were Valentine's Day banners everywhere. It was also the time for the Chinese New Year – there were Chinese banners everywhere, and screens with "Kung Hu Hoch Hi" (Happy New Year) in Chinese written on them. Mahesh was shooting the movie *Gumrah* in Hong Kong. He rented big suites in the Empress Hotel. That morning we went to the place where Mahesh was shooting his movie. He was shooting on the terrace of Ocean Terminus, in a wide-open space. As soon as we arrived on the terrace, a beautiful girl in full makeup came running to us. Someone was calling out, "Sridevi, Sridevi." Then we understood. She was the famous movie actress Sridevi. She came to UG and was saying something to him with folded hands, "It's all right, it's all right," UG was reassuring her. A year ago, that movie star had promised to fix a place in Chennai for UG to stay and then forgot to do it. That caused a lot of hardship for UG. Mahesh probably came to know of it and scolded her. Meanwhile, she realised that her forgetfulness had caused a man like UG many hardships and had been dreading to face UG all this time. Today, she apologised to UG with folded hands for what had happened. She wouldn't quit apologising no matter how much UG tried to calm her down. Mahesh finally succeeded. In a little while, the shooting began. Sridevi hopped and danced with the "horse-mouth" Sanjay Dutt. We watched their running and hopping around for about an hour and left the place. Then, we went to the Swinden Bookshop. Henry was its manager. We all had a group photo taken with UG on the terrace of Ocean Terminus with the background of the Hong Kong Skyline. It was quite a chore to get copies made of that photo. It was included in the photos of the book *Natural Man*.

* * *

In those days, UG was keeping Julie at a distance. That means Julie's torture had already begun. If Julie wanted to stay with him any longer in Hong Kong, Singapore or Tokyo, UG demanded that she must pay him USD10, 000 per day. She agreed to this condition in everyone's presence. Then she was to pay interest on top of that; and she was also to bear the expenses of us both in Hong Kong. To satisfy the conditions of the agreement, she transferred more than USD100, 000 to UG's account. Since then, UG doubled it, thereby, helping her save the money and then returned it to her.

* * *

"The body has no death..."

It was October 7, 1992, the day when UG's camp in Yercaud began. That afternoon, the sun was not very hot and we sat under a tree in the mild sun. The cottage was all wet due to the previous rain. UG was speaking to us about the intelligence of the body.

"The body has no death at all. When once the separateness is gone, the body doesn't belong to you. It's no more *your* body. It's everybody's. First of all, where is the body? There are only certain points of contact. But I cannot complete the picture of my body inside of me by connecting these contact points. So, I have no way of knowing the body," said UG. He waved his hand in the air: "Whose hand is that? Where is the movement? There is no division at all. There is no division such as waking and sleeping. And I don't have dreams."

We finished our lunch sitting under the tree. UG ate a bit of the potato curry–leftover in the refrigerator from yesterday. He also ate a small bowl of *masur dahl* soup that I had prepared. Major ate his sprouts.

Birds were chirping on the tree. The woodpeckers' rhythmic sounds were heard in a distance. UG was silent. No one spoke. I broke the silence and asked him: "They say that there is some

Stopped in Our Tracks

sort of energy concentration in geometric shapes and forms like pyramids and pagodas. What is your experience, UG?" He didn't reply. He was looking at his palm and the lines on it. Suddenly he said, "All the lines in the palm are converging at the Jupiter mount. The heart line, the head line and the life line–all the three are going into the index finger. There are stars coming up on all the mounts. This fellow has a long life line. He is going to live for a long time. He is not going to die in the place of his birth."

* * *

Exorcising spirits...

On October 14, I finished the registration of the Trust and arrived in Yercaud from Bangalore. My old friend Rajaram came with me. He had been suffering from an illness for a long time. He maintained that some "spirit" had been tormenting him. He had had this problem ever since he was with Purnananda Swami. The Swami had tried to exorcise that sprit, but to no avail. Rajaram was hoping that UG could help him. "Some spirit or ghost torments me, trying to free itself. I sought the help of many people–the Swami of Melkota, Swami Purnananda Tirtha and others. But none of them succeeded. My health has been deteriorating day by day," said Rajaram in Yercaud. UG didn't say anything in reply. After a while, he said, "You came to the wrong man. You will be stuck with two spirits instead of getting rid of one," he said. Rajaram failed to understand. "You should stop meditating," UG said later.

* * *

That night, Vedam Satyanarayana and Sashidhara recited the Veda (October 10, 1992) in the South Wing. They recited *Taittiriya*, *Arunam*, *Namakam*, *Chamakam* and *Purusha Suktam* in UG's presence. This was the first Vedic recitation in Yercaud. "During the entire recitation, I felt in my consciousness as if a frustrated attempt was being made to launch an airplane into the air," said UG.

On October 15, 1992, as we were driving to the Shevaroy Temple, UG said, "Today I experienced a strange thing. Hundreds and hundreds of faces marched past in my consciousness. All faces. It's very strange."

"You are like the pig, the dog and the rat. Elephants learn words. And they respond to those sounds. What's so marvellous about language? You're also like those animals, just repeating whatever you have heard. Other than that, there is nothing original."

* * *

A Short Dialogue with UG...

It was October 15, 1992. It was night time. In the South Wing, the Malladi couple, Gita, Suguna, Major and I were present, where UG sat on the sofa. Sanjivi was kindling the fire in the fireplace. It was very dark outside. All was quiet. The following dialogue took place at that time:

Q: UG, nobody has succeeded in describing you. How do you describe yourself?

UG: I have no way of looking at myself. I have no image. There is nobody here. When I say "there is nothing there," it doesn't mean, "*sunya*" and all that rubbish. When I say "it cannot be described," it doesn't mean there is something which cannot be described. There is nothing. Again, some clever chap asks, "How do you know there is nothing?" It's a school boy's logic. I really don't know. It's just a response to your question about my statement that there is "nothing." To say "I have no way of knowing" implies there is something. No. I don't mean that. It has realised by itself that there is no way. Full stop. Period. There is no further movement.

I am describing your state, not mine, your body, your organism. I'm describing the way your body would function when it is freed from the stranglehold of thought.

Q: What is your message to the world? Do you have any?

UG: Why are you so concerned about the world? Are you really interested? Your interest lies in your fears, your security and your relationships. That's all. I have no message for mankind. I'm not interested. Humanity can go to hell. I don't care.

Q: What do you want to put across to the world through the mass media?

UG: I am questioning the whole basis of human thinking. I am brushing aside all that has been built on the foundation of human thinking. My attack is not on religious thinking alone.

Q: Why do you single out religious thinking? How is it responsible for all the ills we are facing?

UG: Everything we think, including the political and legal codes of conduct, springs from religious thinking. They are all the warty outgrowths of the religious thinking of man. All your desire to find the origin of the universe, your efforts to find extra-terrestrial intelligence, springs from religious thinking.

Q: Why do you attack science and technological progress?

UG: Where is the progress? Of what use is that progress? Why is only two per cent of the population benefited by the technological progress? Why is there poverty and hunger? You may pat your backs saying what great progress we have achieved in the field of technology. It took days for our forefathers to cover a distance, which we are now able to cover today in a few minutes by air travel. But how many planes do we use for travel and transportation and how many do we use to destroy the life and property of people?

Q: Do you think the world will benefit from your ravings?

UG: Not a chance. I have no illusions. Take it or leave it. Better leave it. You'll be better off if you leave it.

Q: You want to project that you cannot be fitted into any framework. You're hopeless!

UG: I'm giving you hope here and now. But you are ducking and pushing it off until tomorrow. That's why I say, go to your gurus. They are your comforters. Don't come to me. You cannot have all this and heaven too! You will lose all that you hold precious to yourself. Your wife will go first... You cannot be interested in what I'm saying.

Q: What about your advice to hold on to physical comforts? And what about your talk of money?

UG: In that framework, that's the only thing that you can do. Nothing exists beyond that. If you don't do that, you'll be miserable. For me money is not for security. It's only a means to buy comfort. It's not so for you. For you, it gives security for tomorrow.

Q: You say that the body has its own intelligence...

UG: Your acquired intelligence is no match to that.

Q: Are there two?

UG: No, there is only the intelligence of the body. Acquired intelligence is a myth.

Q: So, one has to leave everything to that fate.

UG: You don't act as one who has trust in that fate. It's not operating in your life. My words are true and valid to me. If you repeat them, it's no use. They're not valid for you.

* * *

He cancelled his trip....

It was October 21, 1992. UG was set to travel to Bombay with Mahesh. The plane was supposed to leave at 4 p.m., but just at that time the plane had a flat tire. UG had already obtained his boarding pass by then. As soon as UG was out of sight moving in the line for security check, we all returned home. Soon after we arrived at home, UG appeared at the "Poorna Kuti" gate in a taxi. "They said it would take another hour-and-a-half for the plane to leave. I tore up the boarding pass and threw it in the face of the official and got out." Later, UG arranged to send Mahesh by another plane. "I didn't want to go. I don't know why, but this time I don't have a mind to leave Bangalore," UG said. His going to the airport and returning–it had never happened like this before.

Vedam Satyanarayana told us later: "Normally, the day that UG decides for travelling is auspicious. The day of the week, the day of the month, the zodiac sign – they would all give him planetary support. It's not premeditated, but if UG decides on a certain date, he won't face any obstacles. But this time, the day he wanted to travel was governed partly by the constellation Aslesha, which is said to be a *Vipattara* [*a constellation which causes calamities*] and partly by the constellation Makha, which is said to be a *Naidhanatara* [*a constellation which causes death*], both in reference to UG's birth constellation Punarvasu. Somehow UG cancelled his trip and the danger has now passed," said Vedam. He said it would be better if UG postponed his journey till January 1993. But will UG heed to this advice? Still, it's strange that it happened this way this time."

* * *

Some incidents...

In 1992, UG was in Mysore for Diwali. Diwali was on October 24. You could hear the sound of firecrackers out on the street. They were exploding intermittently with a huge sound. UG sat in the *verandah* of Brahmachari's house. "Whenever firecrackers explode, I get startled with fear like a small child. The realisation that they're only the sounds of firecrackers would dawn slowly. Still, each time, I startle with fear," said UG.

* * *

A questionnaire came from the International Biographical Centre in UK. It looks like that centre is trying to include UG in its book of *Who is Who*. But you must pay them some money. "I'm sorry; I've never filled out a questionnaire. I don't care whether anybody recognises me or not. This is the man and this is the way he lived and died. Take it or leave it," UG said. He then tore up the questionnaire.

* * *

The next morning, UG sat on the *verandah* in a chair, pushing his feet against the pillar. "There is no body consciousness at all. There is no UG resting in the chair. This foot pressing against the pillar – that's the only UG; there's no other division. This is the only division I am talking about," UG said.

* * *

"Wife and money are the two symbols of security," said UG. "I bring them into focus so that you understand... If you repeat what I say, you are only preventing something that could happen to you," he said. The next day he asked Suguna to stay over in Yercaud. I ended up having to go back to Bangalore alone. I was struck with tremendous fear and anxiety. I felt as if I had lost something. I felt I was becoming alien to myself. During the whole bus travel that same hell, the same torture continued. There was intense turmoil, pain, in myself, in my consciousness. – I wrote about all this. But then, how did I forget all that pain?

* * *

On October 25, 1992, we were in Mysore. That morning Brahmachari arranged for Vedic chanting. I thought Sashidhara and Satyanarayana were perhaps there to do the chanting. Suddenly UG stood up rubbing his palms. "The nerves in my palms feel like they will explode. I wonder why I feel that way?" he said, "They talk about the bleeding in some Christians' palms as a miracle." "Then, why just in palms?" "I don't know. Maybe because they have some important nerve plexuses," said UG.

UG bought Brahmachari new clothes.

* * *

More incidents...

That day, that is, November 1, 1992, we all went to Gandhi Bazaar. Usually, UG buys fabrics in Sanmohan Textiles and Bombay Dyeing. Sometimes he shops in Siddhoji's shop. Then he goes to Sankar Tailors. He gives the fabrics to Sankar to tailor his clothes. That day he said suddenly that we should go to Vedam Satyanarayana's home. When he saw UG getting out of Major's Maruti car, Satyanarayana was flattered and amazed.

"Have you finished your *puja*? Hope we're not interfering," UG said. Satyanarayana, who had been getting ready for his *puja*, said happily, "Why all that *puja* when God Himself has appeared, Sir?" "When that God goes, I also go along with him," retorted UG instantly.

"I can't do that, Sir. God won't go for me," said Satyanarayana and prostrated himself before UG right there and held his feet in spite of UG trying to prevent him. Our eyes moistened watching the scene. "This is all I can do, Sir," said Satyanarayana with tears in his eyes.

* * *

Only two Andhras gave the message of "Go to hell" to the world: one was Chalam and the other, UG.

* * *

November 2, 1992. We were all in the room on the second floor of "Poorna Kuti" with glass windows. That night there was torrential rain. The power was cut off. We all sat around UG in the dim light of candles. At that time, the Mayya couple was present. After she visited UG the previous day, Mayya's wife experienced a miracle. The knee pain she had been suffering from for the last six months had suddenly disappeared. Before that, many doctors had unsuccessfully done different kinds of therapy for her pain. She was wonderstruck that the pain was wiped out without a trace. That night she reported her experience to UG.

Mohan, who was right there, asked, "Then why can't you heal Suguna's headaches, UG?" "Are you ready to take on her headache?" UG chided him. "I suffer with the suffering man; and I am happy with the happy man. Everything around affects me. That's all. There are no healing powers," he said.

Major then started a discussion. In a letter to UG the Princess of Hanover wrote there was a mention of a young Bavarian village woman who had read the lines in UG's palm and said that he had healing powers.

* * *

On November 20, 1992, UG called from Geneva, Switzerland. He had arrived there from India. He went there solely to renew his passport. Ever since the time of India's Independence he has been renewing it outside of India – that means for about 45 years. Earlier, he had a British passport. After Independence, when he was asked to choose between British and Indian citizenship, he, along with J. Krishnamurti, chose Indian citizenship. "Because of my Indian citizenship, I have an Indian passport. I've only gotten troubles and no benefits from the Indian passport. Every time I have to go abroad, I have to get a visa. I must renew the passport every ten years. They always raise some trouble in those embassies for no reason," UG complains.

This time, however, as soon as UG stepped into the Geneva Indian Embassy, a Punjabi Vice-Consul called Kaul welcomed him with respect, seated him and while UG waited, filled out all the forms, got him to sign them and issued him a new passport. He extended the expiry date for ten years, till the year 2002. "I don't think I'll live longer than that," UG quipped. "Please don't say that. You must live for a long time. I've read your books, and I saw your interview in the Doordarshan when I was in Delhi. You must keep coming to Switzerland as long as I am a Vice-Consul here," urged Kaul.

* * *

Some Interesting Things I Noticed in the *Kathopanishad*

"What's the most amazing thing in the world?" a *yaksha* [*a semi-divine being who is half-god and half-demon*] asked Dharmaraja in the *Mahabharata*. Even though his tongue was parched with thirst and his four dear brothers lay by his side appearing dead, he answered unperturbed, "Although man sees countless people dying around him, he lives with the confidence that he will be alive forever and will not die soon. What else is more amazing than this?"

This very thought that amazed Dharmaraja obsessed the terrified seven-year-old boy Nachiketa in the *Kathopanishad*.

Nachiketa realised the miserliness of his father when he noticed that he was giving away Brahmins infertile old cows as gifts in the sacrifice of "donating-all". He could not tolerate his father acting in such a mean fashion, driven by greed to attain the worlds of bliss by "sacrificing everything".

Nachiketa was possessed by the thought, "Why should a person who cannot give away everything perform a sacrifice at all in the first place? Whom is he trying to please? Whom is he so afraid of that he must warp his life in this fashion and deceive himself?" He knew for sure that the high states which his father was hoping for could not be obtained through such deceit.

"Whom will you give *me* away as a gift?" he teased his father. His father got vexed with his pestering and answered in anger, "I'll give you to Yama [*Death*]; just get out of my way!"

Nachiketa thought that his father said the right thing.

He wondered, "What will Death do with me?" Death may have some use for old barren cows, but what use would he have of him? All his ancestors had lived like his father. As grains ripen, fall on the ground and sprout again, so were they born and they died. Must he too go on existing, being born and dying?

He knew he too must die some day. Instead of rejecting and foregoing the opportunity out of fear, he could indeed try to find out the mystery behind life and death by confronting Death willingly.

No sooner had such a thought arisen in his mind, Nachiketa's faith skyrocketed. The spirit of inquiry latent in him for so long was suddenly kindled.

He was transformed in one moment. Breaking all ties and burning like a garland of flames, he arrived at the abode of Yama like the world-consuming Vaiswanara. Consumed by his own fire, for three nights, Nachiketa went into an initiation at Yama's abode.

Upon his return, Yama noticed and was amazed at the intensity of Nachiketa's faith, which stood steadfast in his discipline even in the face of Death.

Then starts the real story of *Kathopanishad*. Only he who has faced death is the seer of truth. Until then that person understands nothing.

Any prophet or wise man becomes enlightened only after arriving at the mortal limits of life. Only because it is the teaching of Death in person that the *Kathopanishad* sheds ever-new light and appears ever so fresh after so long a time.

"First the "you" in you must end. Unless you end it literally, there is no solution to your problems. Until then you won't understand the truth," says UG again and again.

Who cares about solutions after one is dead? Who will understand? What will remain? These, indeed, were also the questions that arose in Nachiketa's mind. He prevailed on Death to answer just such questions.

"First die and then find out. Then there won't be any questions, because then the questioner disappears. The question is not different from the questioner. They are the same. It [*the question*] splits itself into two and carries on the game," UG says.

We sit on one shore and while away our time speculating about the opposite shore.

"First, you jump into the stream. You don't need to be afraid that you can't swim. Don't worry if you are washed away," says UG. (The example in the Upanishads is a leaky boat.)

If we do indeed jump into the stream, then the other shore we have been imagining and dreaming about disappears. Where is the question of reaching it then?

"What will remain then?" asks Nachiketa. Yama, in great compassion, tries to enlighten his pupil. To show that such a question is not inappropriate in such an Upanishad, he points to all the fears hidden within us behind that question.

He explains that it is only because of our separation from this infinite stream of consciousness that these sorrows, problems and stifling questions constantly torment us.

If not in every verse, in many places, you can hear UG's voice in Yama's words.

When you hear Yama repeatedly emphasising, "This is not even a state of mind. This is physical. It's a strange bodily state," you can't but feel UG's presence.

Why should I write specially about *Kathopanishad*? Is it to declare that what Yama says and what UG says are one and the same? If anyone questions, "Who will benefit from this?" true, who will? I moan saying that it has no use.

"How does this benefit even you?" I hear UG mocking me.

How did I come to know about *Kathopanishad*?

I don't even have an elementary knowledge of Sanskrit. I never bothered to study the Upanishads even superficially.

"Why do you bother with this *Kathopanishad* in the first place? Why don't you just live simply?" I tried to talk myself out of it in so many ways. But I could not release myself from its grip.

* * *

It all started when UG came to India unexpectedly in September, 1994. At that time, when UG and I were staying in Yercaud, Mahesh called on the phone from Bombay.

"What's the story of *Kathopanishad*?" he asked without any preamble.

As I was familiar with Mahesh's abrupt ways, I answered right away as well as I could.

Mahesh was writing something on the topic of death. Apparently J. Krishnamurti mentions the *Kathopanishad* in one of his talks.

Mahesh said that Nachiketa had not succumbed to the temptations posed by Yama, but pointed out to Yama instead, "When you are standing behind all those things, what would I have to do with them?" Mahesh wanted to know more details of the story.

After I hung up the phone with Mahesh, my mind started reviewing the details of *Kathopanishad*. I remembered the things in it that caught my attention and wrote them down.

* * *

In the first chapter, 16th verse, Yama says to Nachiketa, "I give you as a gift this necklace with gems of varied colours. Wear it."

What is this necklace? Why did Yama give it to Nachiketa?

You can't find satisfactory answers to these questions in any of the commentaries. Even Sankara merely speculated that "it may have been a necklace with nine types of precious stones, symbolising the maturing of *karma* from many lifetimes."

This gift became physically manifested, one hundred per cent, only in UG's case. After his 'Calamity', among the changes that had occurred in his body was the appearance of blood streaks of different colours in the shape of a necklace, stretching from his neck to his chest. The fact that the swellings were in the form of medallions and appeared like a necklace of nine gems gives a silent confirmation to that verse.

When I mentioned this matter many years ago to Dr. Ramarkrishna Rao, he too was amazed. Then I forgot all about the *Kathopanishad*.

But this time it hasn't let go of me. I have been feeling it as if the lasso of Death has been whirling around me, regardless of whatever activity I am engaged in. I came across other writers' discussions in books on the *Kathopanishad*.

One day, Vedantam Satyanarayana lent me the book *Kathopanishad* written in Kannada by Satchidananda Saraswati Swami. In it there is a wonderful Kannada translation of the Sanskrit original and of Sankara's commentary on it.

Then, one after another, I came across the talks of Chinmayananda on the *Kathopanishad*, a book written by T.V. Kapali Sastry called *Light on the Upanishad*, Krishna Prem's book called *Yoga of Kathopanishad* and the translation by Swami Sarvananda, published by the Ramakrishna Mission in Madras.

I was surprised that I couldn't find the meanings that I had thought of when I read the original text in any of them. I started noting down the thoughts that had occurred to me. Finally, on December 1, I had a strong urge to write down what I had been thinking about the whole *Kathopanishad*, verse by verse, chapter by chapter.

Was I competent enough to do it? I didn't wait to answer that question. From that day on, in exactly 15 days, I completed the writing.

When I finished it and read it over, I felt that I needed to polish it in some places. On the whole, I am glad that I was able to unburden my head of all those thoughts.

I am not concerned about whether it will see the light of day or not. I have faith that if there is any truth in the light I had seen, it will find its own destiny.

UG's words, "If there is any truth in my words, they will stand on their own. They don't need any support," are my guideposts.

* * *

I have a small appeal to make to those scholars who spurn it while turning its pages, saying, "What did he write? Who cares about all these? How is he qualified to write on the subject? What authority does he have to write a commentary on the *Kathopanishad*?"

When I was commenting on the original Sanskrit *mantras*, I tried to stay as close to the source as I could and not to stray from them; I commented on the original words first and wrote their symbolic meaning separately.

As I was only focusing on parallels with UG's ideas in the Upanishad, I didn't consider other commentators' opinions or ideas. Wherever I felt UG's thought was different from Yama's, I noted that explicitly without hesitation. However, I am not proposing or defending any theory in my writing. I feel that Dr. Ramakrishna Rao, in giving the title, *Illivadavilla, Iruvudellaveda* for his first book on UG, published in Kannada, represented UG's thoughts accurately.

"Then, is there such a thing as UG's philosophy? And, do you understand it?" If you stop me and ask such questions, I would answer both "yes" and "no."

If I don't feel that there is a philosophy or that I understand it to some degree or other, I wouldn't need to write any of this. So, my answer is "yes."

But since the truth is something that cannot be reached by the mind or imagination, since UG's teaching is not what we think or experience about it and since there is no question of understanding it, my answer is "no."

I only appeal to you to please set aside all the commentaries and glosses you have read and heard of before and try to look at Yama's teaching from this point of view.

UG says that the root cause of the restlessness and disturbance that have been raging in man from times immemorial, and the anarchy and lack of peace which we are observing all over the world, stem from man's thinking that he is a self and his separating himself from everything else.

Everything is a limitless infinite vibration of consciousness. It's impossible to know how man has separated himself from it as an "I" and built a cocoon around himself.

Although he has thus become separate, his yearning is only about how to achieve union with the whole. But the more he exerts himself and the more he continues to think, the stronger that separation becomes, but does not disappear. There is not a single effort he has not put forth to that end, not a method that he has not pursued or path that he has not followed.

If that separation has to go, it would indeed be death, literally, physical death. That is so because it is thought that has given us a shape as something separate from the universe and maintained our existence as "ourselves". Unless the thing called "thought" is burned away, unless its continuous linking is broken, there is no release.

Then what is the way? How can this separation end? As soon as one points to something and say "this is the way", that way becomes another basis for that separation to continue.

That's why UG says there is no way out. "To know that there is no way is the way." "*Nanyah pantha vidyate'yanaya,*" says the scripture.

Indeed, the mind doesn't admit defeat so easily. There are no tricks unknown to it. That's why no matter how many ways one tries to dismantle it, the framework of separation will carry on inevitably.

So whatever happens must happen in the physical realm. That means there must be unimaginable changes in the physical processes to the extent that there is no scope for the framework of separation to take root. The body, which has been born with thought, must be burnt out and must go through another divine birth. Truth will only dawn then.

Yama explains this same truth in many ways, from different angles. But he also digresses frequently from the essential subject matter and teaches useless trash, as a school teacher recites morals codes. Soon after, either he becomes conscious of himself or is woken up by Nachiketa's shaking him. Then he resumes his profound discourse.

I feel, however, that the principle, which both Yama and UG declare with their liberated voices, is one and the same:

Nayamatma pravacanena labhyo
na medhaya na bahuna srutena
Yamevaisa vrnute tena labhyas
tasyaisa atma vivrnute tanum svam.

[This Atman cannot be attained through teaching
or through intellect or various scriptures.
It's attained by him whom It chooses.
This Atman reveals itself to him.]

* * *

UG and the Upanishads

December 23, 1994

The Kannada friends in Bangalore are to be congratulated for releasing on July 9, 1978, on the 61st birthday of UG, B. A. Ranganath's Kannada book, *Illavadavilla – Iruvudellaveda*, as the first publication on UG. Dr. K. B. Ramakrishna Rao had written an excellent preface to that book.

What is UG's teaching? He says there is none. True.

"His very words are an *Upanishad*. His words frequently echo the Upanishads. Here [*in UG's teachings*], Yajnavalkya, Uddalaka, Aruni, Sanatkumara and the Rishi from *Mandukya Upanishad* – they all gather and reveal their mysteries. Budha, Gaudapada and Sankara – all thrust themselves forward. To those who do not understand, UG's teachings appear strange. But those who can are overjoyed by it, as though their hearts have experienced an indescribable truth, as though their lives are fulfilled." Only someone like Professor Ramakrishna Rao, who is well versed in Vedanta, can connect UG's words with the philosophy of the Upanishads in this manner.

What does UG say about the Upanishads? Does he accept

their philosophy? This is a question that those who are not well acquainted with UG's philosophy ask.

"Why are you concerned about my opinion? I have opinions on all matters–from disease to divinity. I don't care if you accept or reject them. Even the maid in your home has her own opinions on politics, social systems and about many other things. My opinions are no better than those," says UG. He is not saying this merely to brag about his broadmindedness. This is something which no one can believe unless they see firsthand how he practices what he says literally and how he values everyone's tastes and opinions.

In UG's view, culture and tradition weigh down human development and progress. Mankind cannot be free unless it gets rid of them. The root cause of today's political, scientific, economic and social crises, according to him, is the religious thinking that began centuries ago.

The day when the universal consciousness surged forth spontaneously, aroused the consciousness of "I" in itself, and separated itself as an individual consciousness, which enjoys divine experience, that was the day when mankind's peril had started, says UG. Ever since then, mankind has been walking with closed eyes, trying in vain to remove that division and become reunited with the infinite consciousness and has thus been moving closer to total devastation.

"What you see in the Vedic *mantras* and the sayings of the Upanishads is nothing but the struggles of those sages to reunite with the universal consciousness dancing in their consciousness," says UG. That's why in the Vedas there is the worship of the natural forces behind the five elements and of the *lingam* as a symbol of universal energy.

For centuries, different religions, cultures and civilizations in the world have been trying to bring about a change in the beast-like human being and reform him into a nobler being. But only his demonic nature has been gradually on the rise. And why is that? Every popular leader preaches only ideals, shouting "peace", "virtue" and "justice"; but it is rare that anyone thinks deeply about what all this business is about and how it has gone awry. I think the source of man's problems is his effort to fight battles in air while escaping from realities.

"The organism, which vibrates with life, and thought, which is lifeless, is two separate things. There is no relationship between the two. The body only knows how to respond to stimuli and sensations. Thought is something that tries to "experience" them through the veneer of the culture it imposes upon them. Experience, whether it is spiritual or otherwise, is based on the search for pleasure. As soon as it [*thought*] finds something "pleasurable", the desire to maintain it forever arises. The body is not concerned about pleasure and pain. As soon as the limited duration of those experiences is over, the organism pushes those sensations out of itself," says UG.

There has been no change in human nature for thousands of years. No matter how much man has learned or disciplined himself, any transformation that occurred has only been superficial. The beast in man has continued undisturbed. That is the conflict in everyone, the unsustainable struggle that occurs between the animal nature in us and the ideals that our culture has imposed on us. You don't need to ask which side has won the final victory.

"The body doesn't want to learn anything from our culture. As a matter of fact, nature has achieved a great feat by creating the wonderful thing called the body. The body doesn't even *like* to learn anything from us. It doesn't care about bliss and beatitude. It doesn't want any of the pleasures you crave for. It doesn't like anything *you* like," says UG.

UG says that there is no power outside of the body. There is no such thing as the mind, the self, consciousness or the soul. Only the organism vibrating with life exists. That's why UG describes everything that happens to him as bodily experiences.

In UG's view, if there is any effect of the Upanishads or Vedic *mantras*, it's only physiological; there is no effect on any other level.

Swami Poornanadagiri

Towards the end of his stay in Yercaud in the year 1996, a swamiji living in Yercaud visited UG. His name was Swami Poornanandagiri. He was popularly known as the Yercaud Swami. He was a disciple of the famous yogi Jnananandagiri Swami of Tirukkoilur, near Tiruvannamalai. When Major and I first met him in his *ashram*, I was impressed by his simple and straightforward manner. I was amazed at his earnest interest in meeting UG. He said he had heard and known about UG before. He was visibly overjoyed to learn that UG visits Yercaud; and he requested us to inform him when UG would come next. That year, the day before the Sivaratri Day, on February 15, Swamiji came to see UG.

UG huddled into the corner of a sofa, overwhelmed by the musk perfume that Swamiji wore. Swamiji also wore a necklace. We were all astounded by his nodding in agreement to all the contradictory opinions, which UG had been expressing on yoga, meditation, *pranayama* and such. When we were preparing to honour him as a guest, he said with an uneasy face, "Please don't treat me as a guest. I would be happy if you include me as one among you." It was endearing of him to say that.

That day a Canadian called Daniel was asking UG a question. UG suddenly made a profound comment addressing him, "You haven't heard anything in your life; you haven't seen anything. By giving shape to the sounds your ears hear, you think that you are listening and seeing. If you can actually see for one second without that knowledge, your life will end. That's what death is!" Daniel shut up. Swamiji, who sat next to UG, said to Daniel, "Take this as your initiation. You focus on the words which UG has just said and think about them deeply."

After an hour Swamiji reluctantly got up to leave. "I don't feel like leaving such a communion. But I must," he said and looking at UG, "He is a living temple. Why should you spend the Sivaratri in a regular temple?" he said to us.

Swamiji's *ashram* is a couple of kilometres away from the Yercaud Lake. He invited UG and the rest of us to his *ashram*. UG accepted his invitation and we all went there in two cars. Welcoming us at the main entrance of the *ashram*, Swamiji took us into his room. He had also invited a couple of friends from Salem to spend the evening with UG; so we were fourteen in all. We all sat huddled together in that fairly large room. Swamiji tried to get UG to sit on the cheetah-skin seat spread there for himself. UG refused and sat instead in a sofa-like chair. From his nervousness, I could see how happy Swamiji was that UG had graced him with a visit honouring his invitation. UG, on the other hand, was chatting away in his usual fashion without any awareness that he was the chief invitee.

Some stranger came in suddenly, touched Swamiji's feet and was about to touch UG's feet. UG held him by his shoulders saying, "No, no, I never touched anyone's feet in my life. It's disgusting to demean yourself like that. If you want, you can touch your own feet." UG's contention is that there is no power higher than man. "I am clear that I don't have any powers of that sort. Because I don't have them, it's even clearer to me that it's not possible for anyone else to have them either," he said.

Kuppuswami, one of the friends whom Swamiji had invited, was looking at UG for a long time in reverence. "They say that there are treatments which can sustain the body for a long time. What would you say?" he finally asked.

"What's the use of them?" asked UG.

"You can prolong life and not die."

"What's the use? What would you do, living for such a long time?" When UG asked him this question, he didn't know how to answer. Then UG said: "I too say that there is no death to the body, but not in the way you mean. The raw materials that compose the body return to their original state and become newer forms. There is no such thing as 'death' to the body. That's why I say: 'Your birth and your death will never come into your experience.' Then, why do you want this longevity?"

Kuppuswami thought for a while. When he was about to say something like, "There is consciousness in the body...," UG interrupted him, "Whatever you say is the stuff that they put in your head; it's not your own. When there is no such thing as consciousness, what meaning do your words have? ... How do you know that this is such and such? Your touch and your eyes don't say anything about it. You cannot experience even your body except through thought." Then he paused to make sure that Kuppuswami had been following what he said.

Later, for half an hour, he talked about the harm from overeating and told us stories of how the founders of movements like macrobiotics and jogging exercise which have recently become popular in Western countries, while advising us that if we followed their theories we would live long, had themselves died prematurely. We burst into laughter.

"What I am saying after all is that the body doesn't need any vitamins and it doesn't need any proteins. To get all the nutrients it needs, it's enough to eat sawdust. For taste you may add a little glue." When UG spoke like that everyone kept laughing.

"I'm not joking! I said these things even on a TV program in America. Many people argue that they can't believe what I say. But one lady speaking from somewhere in New York said, 'What he says is literally true. When Leningrad was surrounded and they did not allow us any foodstuffs, I ate food items like the ones he has mentioned and I survived. All those years I didn't have a single disease. After I came to this country, ever since I started eating all kinds of health foods, I have been constantly sick.' I don't mean that you should agree with me just like that. As a matter of fact, what do these doctors and scientists know about the body? They don't even know as much as a thousandth part of a mustard seed," he said.

Whatever be the case with excessive eating, the snacks, which Swamiji served us that day, were delicious. Even UG, who doesn't normally drink coffee without cream, appreciated the coffee that day.

As a final item, Swamiji spoke to UG about his health problem. Because of a defect in one of the valves of his heart, he would tire easily. He had difficulty walking or climbing stairs. Surgery was recommended as the only way to correct this defect. His dilemma was whether to undergo surgery or let nature take its course. "If you ask me like that, what can I say? I don't advise anyone. Not that you will find fault with me, but how can I decide for someone else? You do whatever is acceptable to you," said UG.

Later, in another context, UG turned toward Swamiji and said, "If you don't try to practice selfless ideas like love and altruism, the heart does its job mechanically. Only when you practice those things you'll have heart disease." UG thus delivered his irrefutable message. I don't know how Swamiji took this free advice, but toward the end of our visit, when we were about to leave, he heard that UG was quitting Yercaud and said, "There is plenty of accommodation in our *ashram*. There are independent cottages. You and Major can both stay here."

"I have to stay with Major. That's the problem," said UG jokingly.

"That was my intention in inviting Major, too. I know you won't live apart from him," said Swamiji looking at UG. We all laughed at this conversation.

(We later came to know that Swamiji refused to get operated for his heart problem and died gracefully after a year.)

* * *

U.G.'s room...

February 17, 1996 – Saturday, Yercaud

"Sivaratri was last night, not tonight. The nerves around my neck were swollen all of last night; I couldn't sleep," said UG.

In UG's room there is a small skylight. A tiny light peeps through it into the room. Except for that there is no way light or air can enter into that room. In the evening, UG called Sanjivi, asked him to go on top of the roof and cover the skylight. He said that the light bothers him. The room is completely dark now. Besides, there is the heat from the heater.

* * *

Making up...

An item I noted down on January 20, 1997, after Major and I visited Sudha and Chandrasekhar at their home. Apparently, UG had visited their place unexpectedly on December 30, 1996. Sudha related to us how that came about: That same morning, Chandrasekhar went to the Farm House to see UG. Somehow, Sudha came to know of it. She was upset that he went to see UG without telling her. She looked at UG's photo and quarrelled with him saying, "You got just my husband to come there. All right, I'll never see your face again! I don't need you!" Meanwhile, UG asked Chandrasekhar to phone Sudha and tell her where he was. He said to him, "Don't worry. She won't mind." "Talk to her," said UG, and got him to talk to her. He made Chandrasekhar eat with him there. That evening, UG set out on a trip to their home. He went there with the pretext of showing Sudha the greetings Ahalya had sent to Major. She didn't imagine even in her dreams that UG would come to her home. When she saw UG at her front door, all her anger scattered like shreds of cotton fluff.

* * *

Sarvepalli Radhakrishnan and UG

UG spoke many times of his acquaintance with Dr. Sarvepalli Radhakrishnan. I can't remember if I had already written about it all somewhere else. It seems that Radhakrishnan had a great deal of influence on UG in his youth; UG was especially influenced by his oratorical skills. Radhakrishnan was an unequalled intellectual. His lectures demonstrated his eloquence.

In his youth, UG selected three brilliant people as his models whom he wanted to emulate: The first was Sir C. P. Ramaswami Iyer whom UG admired for his versatility. He had a vast repertoire of information; whatever subject matter he was asked to speak on, he had the ability to lecture on it eloquently and discuss it thoroughly. The second person was Sarvepalli Radhakrishnan whom he admired for his brilliance, his dazzling command of the English language, his skill and style of speaking and his torrential phraseology that would astound his audience. And the third was Jinarajadasa who was then the President of the Theosophical Society and who was UG's first spiritual teacher. Jinarajadasa was adept in many languages. He was such an intelligent man that he could speak with unequalled eloquence in about 14 languages from around the world. UG chose the last one also as his guide.

I remember that UG met Radhakrishnan for the first time only after we got our Independence. I can't remember who accompanied him on that visit. Radhakrishnan had his own house in Mylapore, Madras. That day, while talking about other matters, Radhakrishnan suddenly turned toward UG and asked, "Do you believe in *nadi* reading, sir?" "Why are you asking me? Do you believe in *nadi*?" UG countered.

A long time ago, Radhakrishnan consulted the *Kaumara Nadi*. In the reading it was mentioned that "the subject of this horoscope will become the emperor of India." At that time he was a lecturer in Hindu College in Rajahmundry. "How can a guy like me become an emperor," he smiled to himself. Soon after that, he got a position as an Assistant Professor in Madras Presidency College. That was a high status position. He thought that this probably was what the *nadi* had meant. But soon after, he got the positions of Principal of Mysore College and Vice-Chancellor of Andhra University. "This is the Emperor Yoga. What more could there be?" he thought. Later, along with being appointed as the Vice-Chancellor of Banaras Hindu University, he was elected as the Spaulding Professor at Oxford University. It was in those days that he used to speak in foreign countries condemning Nehru and the progressive policies he had been pursuing. Nehru did not know how to handle Radhakrishnan. So, finally, on Patel's advice, he appointed him as the Indian Ambassador to the Soviet Union. After he assumed office in Russia, Radhakrishnan thought, "This, indeed, is the true Emperor Yoga. If I have come here as the Indian Ambassador, that means the *nadi's* prophecy has come true." It was around that time that UG had met him in Madras.

After that, Radhakrishnan happened to preside over one or two speeches that UG gave for the Theosophical Society.' Once, UG attributed what he wanted to say to Radhakrishnan by ostensibly quoting Radhakrishnan's comments and said, "As our honourable President, Dr. Radhakrishnan, had said…" Even such an unequalled intellectual Radhakrishnan (his main possession was his extraordinary power of memory) was flabbergasted and praised UG as the "learned speaker".

* * *

Many years later, when UG was living in Chicago, probably in 1960, UG met Radhakrishnan again. At that time, Radhakrishnan was the Vice-President of India. He came to Chicago at the invitation of the Indian Association there and was staying in the Congress Hotel. UG knew that the management of that hotel had the practice of sending good-looking girls to their guests' rooms besides treating them to feasts. That's why they used to bill them "hundred dollars plus" rent. UG met Radhakrishnan in the hotel. They talked about their previous acquaintance. UG mentioned the hospitality practices of the hotel. Radhakrishnan couldn't keep from laughing. Then UG spoke to him about the lectures he was giving in the U.S. and showed him the portfolio he had prepared containing clippings of press reports of his talks. Radhakrishnan was impressed. "You're doing a great job here. You're performing invaluable service by educating people here about India and Gandhi and Nehru. When you come to India, you must certainly meet Panditji," he said encouraging UG.

Just as he had hoped, in 1961, when UG happened to be in India, he met Radhakrishnan in Delhi. Radhakrishnan arranged an interview between UG and Nehru. That was the first time that UG had met Nehru and it was the last time, too. "Nehru was such an arrogant ... At that time, there was a revolt in Assam. Nehru made a statement in the Parliament to the effect that he was helpless to stop the bloodshed in Assam. That irritated me the most. I told Nehru to his face: 'You are the head of the state and you make a statement like that! If I were in the Parliament, I would have shot you dead for making such an irresponsible statement!'" Nehru was, apparently, furious. He jumped up and down in anger. "Nobody talks to me like this! I don't want expatriates of this country to come and criticize my government!" he shouted. "If nobody talks to you like this, it's your tragedy. I didn't want to see you or meet you. It's your Vice-President, Dr. Radhakrishnan, who has arranged this interview," retorted UG. Nehru calmed down.

UG says that Nehru looked power-drunk and reminded him of Julius Caesar. Later, when Nehru learned that UG was going to Russia and requested UG to lead an Indian trade delegation on behalf of the Government, UG agreed. Nehru apparently said to him, "If at any time you choose to serve the cause of this nation in any manner, it would not be difficult to make it possible." UG replied, "What makes you think that my services will be available to this country headed by a fellow like you?" We can't even imagine how Nehru took that answer.

* * *

C. Rajagopalachari's comment...

Once, a meeting was arranged in Gokhale Hall in Madras to celebrate Annie Besant's birthday. George Arundale spoke condemning Gandhi and his methods. Then it was UG's turn to speak. C. Rajagopalachari was presiding. UG criticized Gandhi thoroughly in his lecture. After the meeting, Rajaji called UG and said to him in Telugu, "So, as they say that the Vaishnava convert wears bigger stripes on his forehead than the real Vaishnava, if your President Arundale criticized Gandhi with some abusive words, you have exhausted the whole abusive vocabulary in English in your attack on Gandhi!"

* * *

"Go Away!"...

On March 3, 1997, UG called from Palm Springs, his new home in California. He seems to have bid goodbye to the Bay Area. "I don't leave my heart behind in San Francisco," was his refrain. In Palm Springs, he has a cottage in Ocotillo Lodge – Room No. 367. This is the same number as the bus route to the Farm House from the City Market. At UG's doorstep the new doormat greets visitors with a "kind" message, "Go Away!"

* * *

Part II

"If you don't think...?"

March 20, 1997, Thursday

When I heard Suguna saying suddenly, "It seems that my chapter in UG's life has come to a close," I felt as if my feet were restrained and I stopped. I looked at her trying to figure out what she meant. "After Valentine's death, I don't seem to have any role to play in UG's life. Moreover, my misery has been getting worse as your book gains popularity and my name is mentioned by everyone." In a flash, I could understand the problem that has been bothering her. She abhors even to recall some of the incidents in my past life. She is pained by memories of the past. "It all depends on what we think. If we don't worry about them, it'll be fine," I said, not knowing what else to say. She didn't reply. It was clear that my words had no effect on her.

As we continued our walk, my head was full of thoughts. How strange is this thinking! Ever since waking up from sleep till we drop off into sleep again, these wheels keep turning around the axle of thinking.

Once, Major remarked to UG, "Your answer to the question of rebirth sounds diplomatic."

"How is that?" asked UG.

"You say, 'There is rebirth for those who believe in it and there is no rebirth for those who don't believe in it.' Isn't that a diplomatic answer?" said Major. UG apparently smiled in reply and said, "Isn't your existence, that you think you "are", a belief?"

Major was silenced with that reply.

Everything depends on our thinking and believing. The priest when he recites the *samkalpam* [*resolve to perform a religious observance*] asks you to say *mama* [*mine*]. That means that as soon as we say to ourselves *mama*, the merit of the observance will be added to our account.

When I think about it, it seems to me that Descartes, who is renowned as the Father of Modern Western Philosophy, condensed his whole philosophy in the principle, "I think, therefore, I am," with this idea in his mind.

"I exist because I think," thought the French Philosopher.

"If you don't think?" is UG's counter question.

That question didn't occur to the Western philosophers. They concluded that man's existence consists solely of thinking.

The vine of life grows around the prop of thinking. What's there if we don't think? If we think a little deeply, we will find how appropriate that question is.

How can we know what there is, or if there is anything?

When the thinking stops, what can be known and who will know?

> The knowing mind
> the world known
> revealing God –
> all are one!

> One silence
> soundlessness beyond sound,
> The whole which fills everything!

We thus slip into Chalam's poetry in *Sudha*.

* * *

Then how does this realisation that "This is all just an illusion of mere thinking," benefit us? How ridiculous it would be to tell a wailing mother who is holding a child in her lap who had just died prematurely and crying her heart out, "You're merely thinking all this. There's neither death nor birth?" So this knowledge is of no use for applying to everyday life. As a matter of fact, it's of no use at all.

There is no release from this turmoil until the consciousness of "I am" is burnt out. Every person experiences this agony at some level or stage, to some degree or other. How can Suguna escape it either? How can even UG save her?

* * *

UG's friends – snakes and cobras

Two days ago, in the afternoon, we had a brand new guest in "Hridaya Vihar". It was March 18, Tuesday. Around 2 p.m., I was lying on the bed in my room, reading *The Gospel of Sri Ramakrishna*. Aruna, Suguna and Sai were chatting. They had closed the front door to shelter us from the heat of the sun. After a little while, Sai, wanting to go out, opened the door. Outside, a four-foot-long snake turned around because of the sound of the door opening and quickly slid into the sewage canal. Aruna and Suguna said it was a big brown-coloured snake as bulky as an elbow. By the time I came out hearing their shouts, the snake had already disappeared. Perhaps snakes come out of their holes in the earth because they cannot stand the excessive heat in them. There is a mound like an anthill next-door to our house. Perhaps this snake lives there.

A month ago, Sai and I had seen in that same place a big cobra which lifted its hood and scared off two cats which lay there waiting for it. Last year, Major said he had seen a big snake around this house. Vedam Satyanarayana also said he had seen a cobra in the park near our house. Perhaps, it's the same cobra, which appeared to all these people. Archana too recently saw a fast-moving snake in the sewage canal across the street.

I felt like saying to the king of serpents, "UG has not come yet. Please come again when he comes. You can see him then."

I am happy to note that UG's close friends move about not only in the Farm House, but also in the environs of "Hridaya Vihar".

* * *

I am myself a thief...

March 28, 1997, Good Friday

Although it's getting past Phalguna, the sun is not so hot yet. This morning, I felt like listening to a tape of Vedic chanting. The sounds of *Rudram* and *Namakam* were going on in tune. I was sitting in the living room in the sofa in front of UG's photo and listening. Suguna had not gotten up from bed yet. It was still dark outside. You could hear no other noise except the sounds of the Vedic *mantras*. When the tape stopped, however, you could hear the drone sound of the snoring of the gentleman next-door. He has two wives. Each of the wives has a separate room. He has children from each wife. They all live together. Each day, the sound of his snoring comes from a different room.

My attention moved from the snoring sound back to the chanting of *Namakam* on the tape and was engaged in it. I was startled when I heard the *mantram "Taskaranam pataye namonamah"*. In this *namakam* intended to praise the Lord, the *mantra* praises the Lord with the phrase "salutations to the Lord of Thieves". We can explain [*the anomaly in this mantra*] without the help of Vedantins unravelling its hidden meaning. They say you should interpret it as, "You, who steals the hearts of your devotees." UG in the photo in front of me broke into laughter. I didn't want to hear the *Namakam* anymore. To praise the Lord by saying "You are a great Thief," means, after all, that He is quite fond of thieves!

When you hear UG saying "Steal, but don't get caught," repeatedly, you would think that UG applauds those qualities which society condemns in people.

* * *

A Christian gentleman came to visit UG in Yercaud and cautioned him by saying, "There is a threat of burglaries in this place. You should secure things like the TV and VCR," UG answered at once, "I am myself a thief. Or else, how am I able to accumulate things beyond my need?" The gentleman looked at him in shock: "You are a gentleman, a great man. That's why you are able to make such statements," he replied, not knowing what else to say.

"No, it isn't that. I'm not so gentle. How do you think I got all these things? Did I get them from working hard? If there are burglars, I would tell them they are most welcome to take them," said UG and turning to the servant Sanjivi who was listening to the conversation, he said in Tamil, "Your master is also a thief; or else, how did he get so much money?" Sanjivi was almost breathless with joy. The gentleman who had come to see UG took to the road and ran away in response to UG's speech. I swear he never again came anywhere near that house.

* * *

It's not just an idea of UG, but even in his dictionary there is no such thing as "thievery". Ever since he was very young, he has formed precise opinions on such traits which society has legislated against. "I want some money. I'll take it if you won't give it to me," he would say to his grandfather. When his grandfather answered, "You're so young, why do you need any money?" and kept his money in a drawer and locked it, UG didn't find anything wrong in getting duplicate keys made and taking the money he wanted from the drawer. "If you had given it to me yourself, you could have saved me the trouble. If you call this "stealing" that's your problem," he told his grandfather when he tried to preach morality.

"Why should you accumulate things beyond your need? You not only steal the things that belong to everyone and hoard them, but on top of that, when someone then steals things because he needs them, you call him a "thief" and torture him. What kind of morality is that? How is that fair?" UG asks.

Moreover, that same society preaches us to give to charity. "You drop a little something which you can't use to someone and acquire the fame of a being a "philanthropist". How crooked, these moral codes!" scorns UG.

* * *

Once, when UG was living with his family in Adyar, his wife realised that her diamond ring was missing. She suspected that the maid might have stolen it. The maid pleaded innocent. UG's wife thought that this approach was not effective; so she reported the matter to the police. The police arrested that woman and tortured her trying to make her confess. They didn't listen no matter how much she pleaded that she didn't know anything about the ring. When he came home, UG learned of everything and got furious. He scolded his wife and forced her to go to the police and get the maid released. "If the police step into our house once more, I will have to throw you out, beware!" he warned her. She later found that ring, which she thought she had lost, somewhere in the house. UG then forced his wife to give that ring to the servant maid as a recompense for her suffering.

* * *

If one wants to understand from what depth UG is saying, "I don't have anything which I can call "mine"," a superficial acquaintance with Vedanta will not do. "Not just things, even these thoughts are not my own. They belong to everyone. Even this body is not mine," he says. That's why when some of his conversations were published as a book and on the copyright page he wrote, "My teaching, if that is the word you want to use, has no copyright. You are free to reproduce, distribute, interpret, misinterpret, distort, garble and do what you like, even claim authorship, without my consent or the permission of anybody," I think UG set a new precedent in publishing history.

All right. It's OK if he stops at exonerating thievery and thieves. Even if he objects to our hoarding possessions saying that that it's our greed and avarice that are responsible for causing such circumstances in thieves' lives, we reconcile ourselves by saying that such a statement only proves UG's honesty. But when UG speaks about thievery as a major art form and claims that the mega robbers who are highly adept at that art should be given a permanent place in world history as wonderful individuals, we cannot but suspect his artistic taste.

When I notice that the same UG who spurns hero-worship of himself says, "If I have to keep anyone's photo in my room, it will only be Al Capone's," and thus pays great respect to an American mobster, I get furious. Why? Such "gentlemen" are not scarce in India or abroad. Why does UG have such fascination for cheats like that? I don't understand.

* * *

Steal, but don't get caught...

Once, UG was walking with friends in Time Square in Manhattan, New York. Suddenly he felt that a hand was moving in his pants pocket. UG innocently looked at both his hands. And while he was still wondering, "When I have both my hands here, how could there be a third hand in my pocket?" the US$95 in his coat pocket changed hands. UG's friends, realising the situation, shouted, "Thief, thief!" while the pickpocket triumphantly blended into the crowd – all this happened within a moment. UG was impressed by the pickpocket's dexterity. Even though UG hailed the fellow as he went through the crowd – "I'm not going to do anything; come here,"– he didn't respond but continued to run away. UG was disappointed. He recalls this incident now and then, not because he lost money, but because he lost the golden opportunity of honouring an expert pickpocket artist by inviting him to a feast in a five-star hotel. "No amount of money will adequately reward the skill he showed in taking that money from my pocket," UG still says in appreciation.

* * *

A bookshop in San Francisco carried UG's book *Mind is a Myth*. The owner of the shop once complained that two books were most commonly stolen from his shop, "One is the Bible and the other is UG's *Mind is a Myth*." The Bible teaches, "Thou shall not steal," and UG's book teaches, "Steal, but don't get caught." That's why they both disappeared so frequently.

* * *

The burglars should have taken everything...

In this context, I must relate an incident that had occurred when UG came to Bangalore the last time. We waited till the time when, on November 25, 1996, UG had left Bombay for Bangalore, to see if Major would arrive in Bangalore from Nellore [*for receiving UG with his car*]. But he had not. Because Major was not in town to receive UG, Gopal Chawla offered to bring his car to the airport and I tried to prevent him. I hired a taxi and went to the airport to meet UG. By the time I arrived, Gopal Chawla and Radhakishan Bajaj were already there, waiting in Gopal Chawla's Maruti car to bring UG to our home. The plane landed exactly at 8 p.m. As soon as UG walked through the gate, Gopal took his bag and walked towards his car.

(UG strongly objects to receiving any help from others. He hesitates when someone offers a car. In India, if he has to use anyone else's car other than Major's, with the exception of Sudha and Chandrasekhar's car, he feels quite annoyed. Sometime ago in the past, when the engineer Srinivas said he would bring his car, I consented. We went to the station together in his car. That time, UG had come from Madras. He didn't say anything in the car as we drove, but he scolded me after arriving home for using Srinivas's car: "You couldn't get a taxi? What would it matter if you had to spend a hundred rupees? What will you do with the money you saved? Why should Srinivas have brought his car to the station? Don't you know that I don't like such things? They may have a desire to do such services, but I don't like at all to receive others' help.")

So, when he got to Gopal's car, UG turned to me and asked, "How did you come here?" I said I had come in a taxi. Furthermore, it was taxi run by Prakash, the son of Viswanath. "Then I will come in that," UG said promptly. Gopal looked disappointed. What could I do? I tried to prevent him earlier. Major was present at the front gate of the house by the time we returned in the cars back to "Hridaya Vihar". He heard that UG was coming, so he travelled on a bus the entire previous night to arrive in Bangalore in the morning.

After we finished with our greetings and coffees, UG said, "Let's go to the Farm House." We all left in two cars. Major had his cottage locked up for a week before then. (There was a risk of robbery in that area. Some time before, thieves had broken into the Farm House and stole the owners' TV and other possessions. Since then, people didn't dare to rent this house.) He had arranged for three or four young fellows to watch the house in his absence. But when we got to the Farm House there was no one there. We opened the gate and walked in. Major came up to the *verandah* and just as he was about to unlock the door, he hailed me. When we looked at the door, it was clear that someone had tried to break in. The outer lock was hanging loose. But the inside lock which also secured the door didn't seem to be broken. The burglar seemed to have tried hard but had not succeeded in opening the door with some pry bar-like instrument. "You're lucky, Major. The door did not open. Or else, they would have taken all your stuff," I said to Major. Everything inside was intact.

Everyone gathered there by that time. UG came there asking, "What happened?" When he learned about what had happened, he examined the door and said in a disappointed voice, "The door wasn't broken. I would have been happy if they took everything." Major replied, "It's okay if they had taken your things, but I would have lost mine too." "Your things too! They should have taken them all. These thieves seem so inept. What good are they if they can't even break doors and locks?" We couldn't help laughing when we heard UG criticising the inefficiency of the burglars.

"I only appreciate success in any effort. I never pity a loser. After all that trouble, if those guys had succeeded in their job, I would have congratulated them," UG said. I thought that those remarks ought to be included in the principles of modern management and motivation.

* * *

"You said no one will come this far..."

March 31, 1997, Monday

In foregone days, everyone would know the news of UG's arrival before I ever told them. Going always by his fixed schedule, he would come to Bangalore at the end of October or in November, go to Bombay or Mahabaleshwar and stay there for a few days, and then leave for Europe. UG's friends would come and enquire about him as the "UG season" neared. He never came to India except in those months. After Valentine passed away, UG's schedule became erratic. Now, it's impossible to guess when he would come and when he would leave. Even UG doesn't know when and where he will go. When he was here last December as usual, he asked me to write down his travel plans for 1997: all of January in Bangalore, second week of February in Australia, and so on. I was suspicious even while I was writing as to whether these trips would actually happen as he had planned. Before the ink on the paper had dried, his plans were turned around completely. On January 1, he flew directly to London. What happened to Australia and New Zealand? Only disappointment remained for the friends there who had been waiting for him.

People ask me from so many far off places, "When is UG coming?" When I reply, "I don't know," they ask "At least tell us where he is now. What's his phone number?" "Don't give my phone number to anyone. If you give my phone number as before to everyone, I won't even tell you anymore," says UG angrily. When people phone me spending so much money from different countries anxious to know UG's whereabouts, I don't like to tell them, "I don't know where he is or any of those details, please don't ask me," as if I don't care. Observing my uneasiness, UG says, "Why should you feel bothered. If you feel uneasy about hurting their feelings, you place the blame on me. Tell them I forbade you."

Obeying UG's command, I have been saying this already to many people. I have also been writing letters to that effect. But some people's letters pain my heart sometimes. Some read UG's book or translation or watch UG's interview on TV and write to me in amazement asking whether such a wonderful person is actually roaming the earth in flesh and blood. They don't know whom to write to track down UG, so they write to the publishers. And when they don't get any reply, they writhe in pain. Then they run into some friend somewhere who asks them to write to me. How many are such unknown friends who pour out their hearts to me! It's not fair not to reveal UG's whereabouts even to such people.

But then, could all those who want to know UG's whereabouts get to meet UG easily? No, it's doubtful. I remember the story of a couple from Barcelona. They wanted to meet UG after they had read the Spanish translation of UG's first book, *Mystique*. When they both arrived in New York, they were told that UG had gone to San Francisco. Then they went to San Francisco straight away. By that time, UG had already left for India via Hong Kong. The disappointed couple returned to Barcelona. After some time, being persistent, they came to India in search of UG. They were confident that UG would be in India this time. They obtained my telephone number in Bangalore through some friends and called me from Bombay asking where UG was. By that time UG had left for Europe. I told them that he would be in Gstaad and gave them his phone number and address there.

Finally, that summer they were able to catch up with UG in Gstaad. When I heard the story of this couple having to travel all over the globe finally to meet UG in the nearby country of Switzerland, I was reminded of Kalyani's words. She used to say that seeing or meeting UG does not depend on our will. "Only those whom the "tricky Kittappa" [*the nickname she gave to UG*] wants to see can come. They can only come *when* he wants them to come. He pushes a button and then they come to him rushing. If he thinks he has had enough of them, he pushes another button. Then they leave right away, not even knowing why they feel they must go," she would say to me, acting it out.

UG, however, now seems to be going to great lengths in his efforts to escape from the people who come to see him. The last time he was in Bangalore, he prohibited people from coming even to "Hridaya Vihar" to see him. He kept at bay even those grey-haired elderly people who normally come every day to see him, including Bhaskara Rao, Vedantam Satyanarayana and Mohan. Radhakishan used to phone every morning and ask about UG's schedule. He hoped that if he could not come as usual, he could at least find room in a car to go around the streets with UG. But UG has been mercilessly keeping everyone away. By this I am not saying that one couldn't see him at all. "If you want to see me, come to the Farm House. If I am there, you can see me there. But you can't see me here. I won't make it easy for you to see me. I don't need anyone. I don't need to see anyone. If you so need me, that's your *karma*; you come to the Farm House," he says. It's not that he doesn't know how difficult it is to get to that forest travelling 20 kilometres from town.

When they finally go there, at times, UG would have already gone away to some other place, thus disappointing them.

Then there are the rules and restrictions that Major has to follow in the Farm House. He must not serve those who come there anything but water. He must not undertake any hospitality. He must not give a drop of coffee even to Brahmachari. (UG knows that Brahmachari can't survive without coffee!) He shouldn't serve visitors any snacks.

"Could we get food packages and eat here?" asked Brahmachari once, hoping that UG would at least concede that.

"You can't eat inside the premises of the Farm House. If you want, you can go outside the gate and eat there," was UG's amendment.

Exclaiming, "My God, what kind of punishment is this!" Brahmachari got out of there.

To get to that Farm House one must walk two kilometres from the Banneru Ghatta Highway. There is a city bus once every hour or two. Major used to take a few friends in his car and drop them off at the highway. UG said he couldn't do that anymore. "There must be no stink and stench of an *ashram* in this Farm House. The *ashrams* all thrive on the basis of food. If you stop the "food orgies", they will all become deserted," he says, equipping us with the first principle for the destruction of *ashrams*.

"Who will come to you, if you set up so many prohibitions and restrictions and build so many fences around you?" asks Major. UG smiled as if saying, "You will see!"

* * *

That day was December 1. UG and Major arrived at our place "Hridaya Vihar" in the morning. I told UG about some friends who had left town for the Farm House to meet UG. "They would have reached the Farm House by now," I said to him. UG decided to go back, and asked both of us (Suguna and I) to go with him. But what about our lunch? There was no time even to think. We both got ready hurriedly and got into Major's car.

By the time we reached the Farm House we saw the Guntur group and Giridhar inside the compound. They were happy that UG had come back to the Farm House. In a few minutes Venkobarao appeared with his son. After some time Murthy got off from his motorcycle with his wife. By noon, a good-size crowd had gathered. How could we feed them some lunch? No one seemed to worry about this question. "How can UG and I eat without feeding all these people?" Major started grumbling. At last, Suguna ventured to suggest a way out. "UG, I'll prepare *upma* for all these people," she said. UG gave an unwilling nod to her offer. We jumped with joy. In less than an hour everyone was busy eating the tasty *upma* that Suguna had prepared, in whatever plate or leaf each one could find. Soon after that, Dr. Narasingarao and company arrived in two large cars. They said they had already had their lunch, fearing that UG would not allow any eating in the Farm House. Narasingarao couldn't believe his eyes seeing all the people eating *upma*.

Realising that his vow was foiled anyhow, UG asked coffee to be served to everyone!

That evening, after everyone had left, UG looked at Major and said, "You said no one will come this far. Look how many were here today." Then Major raised and joined both his hands saying, "A big salute to you," and walked away. Suguna and I couldn't help laughing.

"No better medicine than spit to heal a wound..."

It was 9 a.m. in the morning on December 2. When we heard the music Major's Maruti car makes when he drives it in reverse, I went to the gate. UG was just getting out of the car. "We must go to the bank today. All those chores must be finished," he said.

"I'll make some coffee, UG, we have fresh cream," suggested Suguna. UG came inside and collapsed in the sofa saying "There's still some cream from yesterday." He got up a little while later as if he remembered something and quickly went upstairs. He has a room there which we had built for him. There is also a bathroom next to it. When UG said he was coming for the previous Telugu New Year's Day, we got the room built in a hurry. We had just moved into "Hridaya Vihar". UG stayed there one other time before we had moved in. At that time, UG, Major and my father stayed on the first floor, while Suguna, I and the rest of us were still in "Poorna Kuti". This time, we were in "Hridaya Vihar" for the entire week that UG was in Bangalore. As we had the bathroom walls washed with colour in a hurry, the colours were fading quickly.

As UG was coming down the stairs and saying, "The bathroom walls are weeping," he slipped and collapsed with a thud on the steps. Luckily he held on to the railing with his hands and a serious injury was averted. When we were worried about what had happened, he said, "Nothing has happened, nothing has happened," and went and sat in the car Major's side. Suguna and I sat in the back seats. After the car travelled a little distance, Suguna noticed his right little toe bleeding and a blood stain on his jacket and exclaimed, "Oh, my God, there is blood!" UG saw the blood and realised that his little toe was crushed when he had slipped on the steps and fallen. There were no medicines in Major's car. While Major was looking for a rag or a swab of cotton, UG said, "I don't need anything," and started applying the saliva that he had taken from his mouth on the area where he was hurt. No sooner had he said, "There is no better medicine than spit to heal a wound," the bleeding had stopped. "Medicines destroy the natural immunities of the body. Look at the animals. When they are hurt, they lick their wounds. There's no better antiseptic than one's own saliva. But the saliva doesn't have the ability to prevent bacteria in the mouth," said UG.

Later, UG again said, "The arrogance that "life as a human being is hard to obtain," must go. Mankind is freed only when it reaches the level of animals. Then even sex will go. It's natural to get the sexual urge with the season. Elephants copulate once in seven years. In some species of spiders, after the copulation, the female spider devours the male spider. Beasts don't even have a problem with sex. But man is very arrogant about the status of his species. That's why he is separated from his true nature and pines for liberation."

* * *

"Is it wrong to carry on in my tradition?"

— *Vedam Satyanarayana*

I went to Vedam Satyanarayana's home unexpectedly. Each time I open the gate of his house and go down the steps, I feel like I am entering a sage's *ashram*. His house is near the Sankara Monastery. It belonged to the management of the monastery once upon a time. After Satyanarayana's family ran into some money, they became its owners. There is a room next to the *verandah*. That's Satyanarayana's "observance" room. You can only get into it through his bedroom. We sat in that room for a long time last night, chatting. He was done with his prayers by the time I got there. Since he retired from working, he has acquired the habit of eating a small snack around 11 a.m. He only has coffee before his prayers. He prays every day for two hours, starting at 9 a.m.

Satyanarayana and I both got acquainted with UG in December 1969. But we had known each other before then. We used to meet in Brahmachari's "Cave" each evening and spend our time discussing spiritual matters. Satyanarayana did his M.Sc. in Statistics. He worked for the National Tuberculosis Institute and retired from the same institution in 1996. In all my thirty years of friendship with him, I haven't noticed the slightest change in his lifestyle. He is still the same and embraces the same beliefs as he did when I first met him. Even though, he has become a householder now; still there is no change in his lifestyle. His appearance also hasn't changed throughout these years: He dresses just like he used to before – in a *dhoti* and a shirt made of coarse cotton. He applies holy ash on his forehead. Except when he goes to his office, he always has this appearance. He prays and studies the Vedas without fail every day. He performs these activities with great devotion. He is a man of virtue. Whenever I observe the faith and devotion he shows in performing his duties, I feel that an ancient sage like Gautama or Vasishta has reincarnated. He is thoroughly versed with not only our ancient myths and epics, but with the whole Vedic literature. That doesn't mean he is a blind follower sold to ancient ways and orthodox customs. My considered opinion is that few people know as well as Satyanarayana how far modern science has progressed. It's enough to look at the books displayed on the shelf in his observance room to know how much interest he has in science.

He used to come with some friends and recite Vedas in UG's presence. Except on those occasions, you would never hear his voice in UG's presence. Whenever he came, he would sit in a corner and spend his time without talking much to anyone or indulging in debates, as much as he could help it. Whenever he came, it was UG who would bring up the subject of his horoscope and make him talk. I doubt if even ten per cent of those astrologers who do business with signs outside their houses know as much astrology as he does. He has always been a loner who is not well known to anyone except to his close friends, of whom there are only one or two.

Those were the days when Major Dakshinamurti started visiting UG. He never could make sense of the Satyanarayana's manner. He could not figure out how such an orthodox and religious-looking person could come to UG and listen to all his heresies. At that time, Major held the opinion that UG was an arch enemy of orthodox tradition. He could not understand how a person like Satyanarayana could reconcile UG's words and teachings with his own beliefs and actions. One day, Major asked Satyanarayana that same question in the presence of everyone. "How could you carry on your worship and observances while still listening to whatever UG says?" Satyanarayana didn't say a word in reply. Noticing his silence, Major satisfied himself thinking that perhaps he didn't want to answer him.

The next day, while Major was cleaning his car, Satyanarayana opened the gate and came inside "Poorna Kuti". "I didn't feel like answering your question yesterday in front of everyone. If you want to hear, I would like to explain myself now," he said to Major, "I was born in an orthodox family. As a child I grew up in the atmosphere of worshipping Gods and the study of the Veda. I inherited these practices. Although I had to work to make a living, I didn't understand why I should discard the traditionally imposed duties. UG doesn't care for them. That's the sort of level he has attained. I don't see the wisdom in quitting them all just because he is condemning them. My worship of Gods, my morning and evening worship and my reciting the Vedas also provide a pastime for me. If I quit doing them, what would I do with my free time? I would have to play cards in some club or gossip with some friends or pick up some other activity. Is it wrong to continue whatever I have been doing all these years instead of starting something new?"

Major did not say a word in reply.

* * *

Fifty per cent of the time...

April 5, 1997, Monday – at the Farm House

Major's brother, Dr. Subba Rao came from Nellore to visit UG early this morning. Major picked him up at the bus stop. He had travelled from Nellore by bus the entire previous night. His son, Dr. Sridhav, had been ill for several months. Many medical tests were conducted in Madras Apollo Hospital. The doctors could not diagnose the illness. Finally, Dr. Subba Rao prayed to UG. Sreedhav then turned the corner. The problem was discovered: one of his ribs broke into two pieces and a bit of his rib stuck in his lungs, causing pain on the right side of his chest. Dr. Subba Rao told UG, "Only your grace has saved Sreedhav, nothing else."

Major said, "It doesn't work all the time and in all cases."

Then UG immediately said, "It's the same even in the scientific field. Their theories don't work all the time. Always, 50-50."

"Do you say your methods are scientific?" asked Major.

"I don't mean that. If there is a God, why would He be on your side just because you are praying to him? What kind of God is He then? He should be on the side of one like me who doesn't pray," said UG.

* * *

Satyanarayana's dream...

April 7, 1997, Monday

Satyanarayana gets strange dreams. He believes in them. He says that the memories of the dreams fade out if he moves in his sleep or lies on his side. He has developed a routine of getting up from bed, no matter what time of the night it is and noting down somewhere those dreams that he felt were wonderful.

It was January 6, 1980. That night he had a dream: UG was sitting on the floor. The setting was the house on West Anjaneya Temple Street. Subbanna Manja was with them. Satyanarayana was reading to UG from some book and discussing the material with him. The content of the book was related to astrology. The scene was suddenly erased. As he was waking up, he felt that someone uttered loudly, "Mind is a Myth" and then said "2, 12, 19." He thought the numbers were perhaps pages numbers of *Mind is a Myth*, got up from bed at once and wrote down the numbers and the current date on a piece of old calendar paper, the only thing that he could get hold of on the table.

Before 1980, even *Mystique of Enlightenment* had not yet taken shape, let alone *Mind is a Myth*. "How could I have such a dream? What about those page numbers?" he wondered and couldn't figure out. But he preserved that piece of paper in some diary and then forgot about the whole thing. Fourteen years passed. In the meantime, UG had visited Bangalore many times and Satyanarayana kept meeting him. Besides Mind is a Myth, many books, videotapes, radio and TV interviews, articles in newspapers and magazines and such have been published. For all these years, Satyanarayana did not remember this dream. One day, when he was browsing through his old diaries, the piece of an old calendar suddenly dropped from one of them. When he read it, the 14-year-old dream flashed at once through his mind. Immediately he picked the copy of *Mind is a Myth* he had on his shelf. It looked just like the book he had been reading to UG in the dream. "Then what about the page numbers?" he wondered and looked up those pages.

* * *

"How could UG's birth be ordinary?"

Till then, Satyanarayana had read pages from the book *Mind is a Myth* here and there, but he had never read the book carefully. On the second page, there was a description of the cover page. On page 12, there was a mention of UG's birth. Satyanarayana saw the following sentences written by Terry Newland in his Introduction:

The subject of this work, Mr. Uppaluri Gopala Krishnamurti was born of middle-class Brahmin parents on the morning of July 9, 1918, in the village of Masulipatam, South India. As far as we know there were no peculiar events surrounding his birth, celestial or otherwise.

Satyanarayana believes that the birth of great realised men cannot be an ordinary occurrence. He does not just believe; he provides innumerable instances to support his claim. Everyone knows that when Jesus Christ was born 2,000 years ago, the bright star that had arisen in the sky in the east appeared and showed the way to the wise men. Similar was the birth of Gautama the Buddha. In the book, *Transforming Light – The Living Heritage of World Religions*, we read:

It is said that whenever a great divine cosmic force descended from the heavens in response to the wishes of the Gods, it made five important choices, viz., the time, the continent, the country, the family and the mother.... Buddhas are born in the continent of India. Buddhas were either Brahmin or Kshatriya family, whichever was high in public estimation.

Further on we read about Buddha's mother as follows:

The remaining span of life of Buddha's mother was ten months and seven days since the time of conception. A womb that has been occupied by a future Buddha is like shrine of a temple and can never be occupied or used again...

That's why Tathagata's mother, Maya, died seven days after the Buddha was born. Just seven days after UG was born, his mother, Bharati, too, had died. While placing her baby in her father's care she said, "This boy is born with a purpose." She was a devotee of Krishna. "These are historic truths. We can't deny them," said Satyanarayana.

According to esoteric beliefs, the Eastern direction where the sun rises is the fountainhead of profound wisdom. One look at UG's natal chart reveals how all the planets are clustered on the Eastern side of the chart. UG's birth place, Machilipatnam [*same as Masulipatam*], is a coastal town in Andhra Pradesh and is located on the Eastern most point of the South Indian Peninsula.

Drawing another parallel from Buddha's life, Satyanarayana read the following lines from the book, *Transforming Light – The Living Heritage Of World Religions*:

Buddha knew (his teacher) Alarakalama's system of thought and doctrine by heart. Buddha asked himself: "Does Alarakalama practice what he teaches? Has he attained the exalted state which he describes?" He practiced Alarakalama but did not find advancement. He left the teacher."

"This is very much similar to UG dismissing JK's authority and walking out on him," observed Satyanarayana.

* * *

Searching for supernatural truths with his inner eye

Then how is it possible that UG's birth was an ordinary affair? On page 19-20 of that book, there is an account of how UG went with Valentine to hear J. Krishnamurti's talk, how the question "Is there enlightenment?" which occupied his mind until then, had disappeared under the tree in Saanen and how that event triggered a series of changes that had ended in the "Calamity" exactly on his 49th birthday. Tathagatha's enlightenment too occurred on his birthday, under the *bodhi* tree.

That day, after Satyanarayana turned the pages in that book, the meaning of the dream he had had suddenly flashed in his mind. "I must publish to the world an account of the supernatural and wonderful truths connected with UG's birth from the point of view of myths and epics and the predictions of astrology and astronomy" – as soon as he thought this, a new enthusiasm arose in Satyanarayana. A determination and resolve unknown to him before had surged in him. It would not be an easy task. It would not be a joke to shake up old brains, stuck in old traditions with stale beliefs, frozen with the fanatical view that there couldn't be anything in the world that they hadn't already learned, puffed up by the great success that science has achieved. Satyanarayana's life's work started that day. He had already studied UG's horoscope thoroughly years ago and recorded the wonderful yogas and auspicious movements of planets he had observed in it. Taking UG's horoscope as the base, Satyanarayana began searching for supernatural truths with his inner eye. Then he gradually began to see new lights and visions before his mind's eye.

* * *

Interpreting UG's horoscope

It was UG's 76th birthday on July 9, 1994. Strangely, UG's birthday that year according to the Telugu almanac coincided with his birthday according to the Western calendar. The constellation that day was also *Punarvasu*, UG's birth constellation. The day of the week was Tuesday. And UG was born on a Tuesday as well. All these coincidences seemed extraordinary. That year, 1994, was Bhava. Exactly on New Year's Day of that year my Telugu translation of *UG Krishnamurti, A Life*, was released in Hyderabad.

One day, I discussed this matter with Satyanarayana. Both of us talked for a long time that day. The things he talked about that day, the divine secrets that occurred to him in examining UG's horoscope, the messages he had heard, the visions he had experienced – all seemed extraordinary to me. We talked in Satyanarayana's room, in the presence of the great souls assembled there (as pictures), about the many strange and wonderful things that have not been seen or heard before.

It's hard to estimate how many people would appreciate hearing about the things that plunged us both into wonder and amazement. I wouldn't even be surprised if people will laugh at them as cock-and-bull stories. However, those who accept astrology to some degree or other and agree that there is an intimate relationship between it and our myths and epics, cannot but appreciate the many ways in which the highlights of UG's life enlighten us with divine truths which have not yet become apparent to us.

* * *

When there is a mention of astrology, UG often says, "I don't believe in astrology. But it will be useful as a good example to those who are knowledgeable in it, if they can examine how, from the beginning, my horoscope has been governed by the influence of the movements of the planets." UG's entire life has run as a mirror image of what astrology has depicted as a result of the influence of great stages and sub-stages of the respective planets. It still does.

Nevertheless, when UG says, "Planets have no influence on my actions and there never will be any," it's quite true. It is only on the multitude of humanity, which has been severed from the infinite consciousness and carries on in diversity that the planets have influence. How can there be a separate existence for great souls like UG who are united with the universal consciousness and who vibrate with limitless life energy? That's why, whatever intentions arise in these minds, they would be consonant with the influence of the planets.

"My actions are responses. They are never reactions," says UG.

I ask that the things I am now going to write about should be examined in this light.

* * *

UG's year of birth is Kalayukti. That's one of the sixty years in the cycle of years in the Indian lunar almanac. The presiding deity for that year is Kalki. When the Sun was in the house of Gemini, that is, in the month of Ashadha, UG was born. Trivikrama is the presiding deity of the month of Ashadha.

Everyone knows about the incarnation of Vishnu called

Trivikrama. The myth tells us the story of how Trivikrama, in order to satisfy the three "steps" of Bali's gift, pushes Bali down to the underworld with his foot as the third step, while with his first two steps he occupies the whole of the animate and inanimate universes. Satyanarayana tells us of the implied symbolism of this in an interesting fashion:

> The emperor Bali was a spiritual aspirant pining for the realisation of non-duality. Vishnu appeared in the form of Vamana. With one of his two steps he filled the phenomenal universe and with his second step he filled the unseen imaginary universe. Then there was no room left for Bali's existence. "Where shall I place my third step?" asked Vishnu. Bali was aware of his existence as separate from the universal consciousness. That's why he asked Vishnu to place his third step on his head that was the basis of his existence. With the touch of Vishnu's foot, the duality in Bali's consciousness was shattered. He was plunged in the infinite ocean of consciousness.

The essence of the incarnation of UG, who was born under the supervision of the God Kalki, is to destroy the division in consciousness, says Satyanarayana.

* * *

Commenting on the coincidence of UG's birth dates [*both Eastern and Western*] falling on the same day, Vedam Satyanarayana said: "This year the planetary situation is very close to that which obtained at the time of UG's birth 76 years ago. If we have to hazard a guess about the nature of things to come, we must first understand the nature of the forces that were unleashed at the time of his birth." He then told me that UG's birth itself was a rare celestial event that heralded the birth of a great force. I knew well that my friend is never given to exaggerations. Precision and veracity have been his hallmarks, be it in his field of statistics or in his hobby of astrology.

I was curious to know how UG's birth created a sensation in the heavens. "You need to fire your imagination a bit to behold the picture I am going to project," said Vedam with a benign smile. His dark serene face glowed as though he was under the spell of some mysterious power.

Imagine yourself standing at the place of UG's birth, Machilipatnam, on the globe. Imagine watching the rise of planetary constellations in the heavens in the same sequence as depicted in his natal chart. A constellation rose in the horizon every two hours. UG's birth took place on July 9, 1918 at 06:12 a.m., when the entire Western horizon was waking up to the new dawn. *Sukra* (Venus) and *Ketu* (the Descending Node) are the two planets that appeared in the constellation of *Vrishabha* (Taurus) in the first two hours of the early morning of UG's birth.

According to Hindu mythology *Guru* (Jupiter) and *Sukra* are two great teachers who laboured to end the divisive consciousness, which is the root cause of mankind's misery. *Guru* symbolises belief, orthodoxy, tradition and long-lasting trust, while *Sukra* symbolises doubt, scientific and investigative approach and an ever-changing temperament.

While *Guru* became the leader of the divine forces ruling the universe, *Sukra*, the one-eyed doyen of the occult powers, consolidated the dark forces and countered the godly forces. Both the forces waged wars against each other for ages trying to establish a unitary force. At last they both realised the limitations of their efforts. Their prayer for the advent of a Universal Force was answered in the birth of UG.

Thus *Sukra* appeared in the *Vrishabha* [means "*the bull*", *the carrier of Lord Siva*] constellation, with a flag of "total emancipation", symbolised by *Ketu*, who is also called *moksha karaka* [*the bestower of enlightenment*]. *Sukra* was in the forefront of the cosmic parade of the planets, heralding the birth of the Universal Force in which divisions have disappeared. Lord Ganesha is considered to be the presiding deity of *Ketu*.

The next constellation to appear in the firmament was *Mithuna* (Gemini), which symbolised the culmination of all dualities. *Guru* (Jupiter) appeared first in this constellation. Lord Brahma is considered the presiding deity of Jupiter. *Ravi* (Sun) appeared next with his presiding deity Lord Siva.

It is believed in the ancient lore that when Lord Siva came down to fight the demons called Tripura *Asuras*, Lord Brahma became his charioteer. The Sun and the Moon formed the two wheels of the divine chariot. *Ravi* in the ascendant is said to be the *Atma karaka* [*bestower of self-realisation*]. In UG's chart, *Ravi* is in *Mithuna* and Moon is in *Kataka* (Cancer), symbolising the two wheels of the chariot driven by Brahma, the presiding deity of Jupiter.

The Ascendant in UG's chart symbolises the Universal Force that had descended in the Mithuna constellation at 29 degrees and 30 minutes.

When *Lagna* [*ascendant*] rises at the end of the *Ravi*, which is owned by the benefic *Guru* that occupies the *kendra* [*square*] or *kona* ["*trine*], *the native is said to attain emancipation in this very birth. He will be an unusual contributor to mankind.* [Ref. *Astrological Magazine*, March 1973.]

In UG's case, *Mithuna* is the ^{lagna}, and the *lagna's* lord *Budha* is benefic. *Guru* occupies *Kendra*, thus satisfying all the above conditions.

According to the Indian calendar, UG was born on the *Ashada Shukla Padyami* [*1st day in the bright half of the Ashadha month*]. In Hindu mythology it is stated that Lord Siva manifested himself on that same day to save his devotee Markandeya from the clutches of death. Siva thus came to be known as *Kalasamhara Murti* [*Destroyer of Time*] who killed Yama, representing "Time", in one stroke with his trident [*symbol of past, present and future*].

The next constellation, *Kataka* (Cancer), rose in the horizon containing Moon, Mercury and Saturn. *Chandra* (Moon), the lord of *Kataka*, symbolises the mind of the Universal Force. Having occupied the same *Varga* [*class*] in six *amsas* [*aspects*], Chandra is said to have attained the *Parvatamsa* [*the aspect of the mountain*], in astrological jargon. Similarly both *Budha* (Mercury) and *Sani* (Saturn) have attained *Gopuramsa* [*the aspect of the gate*] and *Simhasanamsa* [*the aspect of the throne*], respectively. The presiding deity of *Chandra* is Durga, whereas that of *Ravi* is Siva. Both Siva and Sakti become the unifying forces of the ascendant. This aspect bestowed *Ardhanariswaratva* [*the characteristic of being half-woman half-man*] on UG.

According to Indian astrology, each planet has its own distinct energy form called *mandala*. It is said that the energy form of Saturn is the "bow" and that of Mercury is the "arrow". In UG's chart they are in the 2nd house, which signifies speech. The Moon represents his mind-force, which is like an invincible resolute warrior and which is poised to shoot using his words as arrows. *Kataka* being a movable sign, the presence of the three planets keeps him in constant movement.

By the time the other constellation *Kanya* (Virgo) appeared with *Kuja* (Mars), the Sun was in mid-heavens. It is known as *Abhijan muhurtam*, a very auspicious moment for the invincible *Kuja* (Mars) to rise. The indication is that *Kuja* wields his power during the mid-life.

The last constellation to appear with *Rahu* (Dragon's Head) is *Vrischika* (Scorpio). *Rahu* is considered the Durga, *sakti*-power of the Divine Mother, which joined forces at the time of victory. *Rahu* in the 6th place and Jupiter in the ascendant bestow a *yoga* called *Ashtalakshmi yoga*, which keeps the rich and abundant resources of the world at the beck and call of the native.

* * *

"UG is a Volcano ready to erupt..."

– Mahesh Bhatt

April 8, 1997 (Tuesday) – New Year's Day

Today is the beginning of the Year Ishwara. It's evening time, around 8:15 pm. By this time UG must be flying in the area of Hong Kong above the Pacific Ocean. He will arrive in Bombay via Hong Kong on the night of 10th. Mahesh said that he would arrive in Bangalore the next morning on a Jet Airways flight.

* * *

Mahesh conveys UG's message

April 9, 1997

Mahesh called from Bombay. He was announcing UG's arrival. He had spent a few days with UG in Palm Springs earlier. "Babu, I never hated him like that in my life before, including all the past things he had said and stood for. This time I hated him," Mahesh was talking about UG. "He is like an inferno, like a volcano. All the time he was boiling and bursting. He was shouting with total fierceness, 'Mankind should be wiped out from the face of the planet!' He's out to destroy humanity. He's not the same UG that we have known and talked to with fondness. I don't want to be

Stopped in Our Tracks

with him or go near him for anything in this life. Babu, we both, you and I, are the symbols of humanity. He is attacking everything we hold dear to ourselves. "Forewarned" is "forearmed", Babu, be careful! He is again talking of those photos and files. 'Babu should not build his life around me,' is his refrain." That was the message Mahesh gave me today.

* * *

April 10, 1997, Thursday

The things Mahesh has told me on the phone yesterday and this morning are unforgettable. Those words still ring in my ears. I was shocked to hear Mahesh, who would die for UG, who considers UG as his walking God and who values UG higher than anything else, talking as if he wants to run away from UG.

He had just seen UG in the US. He was there in Palm Springs for six days before the beginning of April. Even when he called from there, he frightened me by asking, "Why are you inviting UG to India? You're looping a noose around your neck." I brushed it off telling myself that's just Mahesh's manner. But when he called me from Bombay he talked in the same fashion again: "The UG whom you have been so fondly and lovingly thinking about is not the UG you are going to see now. This is a volcano ready to erupt. This is a fire-face constantly bubbling with lava and burning, ready to destroy the human race."

He continues and says that in each word and action of UG there is a passion and fury demolishing all the edifices of hope that we have built for so many years. "'Instruction through insult' is a lie. How do we know in the first place that UG is enlightened?" When Mahesh talks like this, I feel that a change has occurred not in UG, but in Mahesh. Some unknown change is taking place. The steel citadels inside Mahesh are crumbling and a new energy unknown to him is rushing forth. That is why I think UG now appears to him that way.

"If I can help it at all, I will keep UG at a mile's distance and run away. I can't take UG. I can't," he says, "Forewarned is forearmed,

Babu! Beware! Be careful! You can't imagine. He is stamping with his feet more ferociously than Calcutta Kali. Wherever we try to hide, he drags us out mercilessly, tears us apart and cuts us into pieces!"

I know that UG talks about man's appearance on the earth as the cause of its destruction. My friend is now telling me that a passion is now bursting forth like a conflagration in UG. Those who gather around him are unable to withstand that heat and are running for their lives.

I think it's now becoming evident that UG is truth incarnate [*avatara tattvam*]. I feel this not just from listening to his words for so many years; or taking the blows he has dealt while thinking "this is all for our own good;" or thinking of the Zen masters and comforting ourselves that "we understand, only we don't know that we do;" or thinking that perhaps we have been maturing and thus congratulating ourselves. Now the world will have a taste of UG's power. He is fury incarnate and Narasimha [*man-lion*], the incarnation of Vishnu. In UG, who combines the two, all must be consumed and turned into ashes. There is no escape. This is inevitable. O, world! Beware! Save yourself from yourself, if you can!

* * *

Non-existent Problem...

April 12, 1997, Saturday

Shanta called and wanted to see UG. Ever since she became a working woman, she has been busy with her routine schedule. Her visits to UG have become few and far between. On Saturday, she came to "Hridaya Vihar" with her friend Suneeta. Shanta was dressed in a green *chaudidar* and looked glamorous. As soon as she arrived, she started talking to UG. She looked agitated and depressed. I couldn't figure out what was bothering her. UG sat in his usual chair facing the main entrance. Shanta and Suneeta sat on the long sofa.

"UG, how come I'm back to square one after so many years? You must solve my problem..."

UG did not look impressed. He first tried to stall her by saying, "I don't see any problem there now." But she persisted and said that she did have a problem.

"Go to your gurus for solutions. Why come to me?" UG asked.

"UG, you're of no use. You're the only one who can solve my

problem," Shanta said threateningly. "I seem to be losing my interest in everything. I have no conviction in anything. I have no goals and no purpose in living. I've lost all hope. What's left is only despair. This is torturing me, UG. You must help," she pleaded.

"That's all good for you," replied UG and said nothing more. Shanta then turned to me and said, "Chandrasekhar, I am now 49. You remember, you once said looking into my palm that in my 49th year I would be facing a crisis in my life? I think your prophecy has come true. I have really lost my interest in everything."

Then UG looked at her with a mischievous smile and said, "Nothing is free in this world. It will cost you if we have to solve your problem, your non-existing problem." Shanta answered that she was ready to pay the price.

"Then pay now, cash on the barrel – fifty thousand. I shall settle for rupees because this is India. Otherwise, it would be fifty thousand dollars. If you pay me Rs. 50,000, you will then forget your problem and start thinking about the money you have lost. And your problem is solved!" said UG.

We all burst into laughter. Shanta, too, couldn't help but laugh. For a moment she appeared to be out of her depressed mood and back to her normal jovial self. Then UG talked for a while about the problem of relationships.

Shanta said, "I lost all my feeling for relationships. I feel as if I don't have a relationship with anyone."

"It never existed in the first place," UG corrected her. "When you don't want to let go of a relationship, you use emotion. First of all, relationships are non-existing. You think you have relationships with people around you. You can possess articles, houses or cars. But how can you possess human beings?" he continued, "You use emotions to control people."

Shanta and Suneeta stayed and had dinner that night with UG. I suggested that she should read her own book on UG to get over her problem. Before she took leave of UG, Shanta said, "UG, after hearing you, reading books about you and spending so many years with you, I thought I had understood you. But now, after twenty years, I am back to square one. I have been happy all this time. I thought I had understood and sorted out all my problems. But suddenly I realised that I know nothing. I have lost my interest in life. Save me."

UG somehow seemed to have showed her again that night that she actually had no problem. She left in a cheerful mood.

* * *

Dr. Sudarshan

April 13, 1997, Sunday – Bangalore

Dr. Sudarshan of BR Hills, a man of alternate Nobel Prize fame, came to see UG at 3 p.m. There was a big gathering. UG spoke for about two hours. "The body requires only two "F's", said UG in one context. Dr. Sudarshan looked puzzled. He probably guessed the first "F" as food, but he could not guess the second "F". "What's the second "F", UG?" he asked UG naïvely. He did not expect UG to be so blunt and crude in his approach. When UG explained explicitly the activity for which the second "F" stood, he couldn't believe his ears. While leaving, he received from me a set of all the books on UG for his library in BR Hills. He invited us all to BR Hills. Does UG visit such places? "Do you want me to destroy?" UG asked Sudarshan.

Rangarajan, the "maddie", was here this evening. He told us that he had written to his Master of the Radhasami Satsang recommending that UG be granted the "higher states". He mentioned to UG about his letter to his guru. UG said, "I am ready to take you as my guru, but not your guru." Major interpreted UG's remark and told Rangarajan to behave himself; otherwise, he warned, he would be asked to get out.

* * *

April 16, 1997, Wednesday – Madras

Four of us (UG, Major, Suguna and I) left for Madras at 4:30 a.m. That evening there was a gathering on the terrace of Krishnamurti's house. Rajan came to see UG. Dr. Ravindra Babu from Vizag was also there. UG talked about many things:

"I never have jet lag. I adjust my body clock to the time of destination two days in advance."

"The pineal gland controls the sex impulses and functions of the sex glands."

"Sex is impossible for me. My penis is the size of a child's."

"Karma is not fatalism. It's not genetic. Man is the moulder of his own future and architect of his own destiny."

"I am responding to every situation, whereas you are only reacting."

""*Karma*" means action, action without any reaction."

"I don't need any doctor. The body has enough intelligence to survive. My saliva cures my wounds. Surgeons are like mechanics. Medical technology knows nothing about the body. What they know is immense. But what they don't know is infinite. Still, I tell people who are suffering to go to a doctor. There is no special charm in suffering."

* * *

Facing Yama, the God of Death

April 23, Wednesday

Last night was the full moon of the first lunar month. The moon was showering light from the clear skies. Major's freshly whitewashed cottage was shining in the moonlight like the Taj Mahal. All the coconut trees in the garden stood swaying their heads as if they were bathing in the moonlight. The *koil* birds were clearing their throats now and then sitting on the mango branches preparing for the next morning's performance.

The garden is asleep
hiding in the womb of the river...

Enki and Nayudu *Bava* [*cousin*] [*the two lead characters of the poetic work*, Enki Patalu, *by Nanduri Subba Rao*] flashed in my mind spontaneously. "Will you not love me tonight, my prince?" Enki's plaint resounds in my heart.

There were bright lights in the living room. As soon as I saw UG's form through the bars of the window, feelings of anger, revenge and hostility – all surged in me. Although I abruptly turned around and stood outside the cottage, greeting the hibiscus flowers, I could hear UG's voice sounding like a death knell. There were about 15 people in the living room.

Yesterday evening, Hanumantha Rayudu brought a couple of old friends to my home in a Maruti car. One of the two, Rajaprakash, is the father of the Kannada movie hero Sashi Kumar. They wanted to meet UG. Suguna and I set out with those three for the forest cottage in Banneru Ghatta. By 5 p.m., they were all sitting in the living room listening to UG speaking.

Since yesterday morning I have been experiencing some disagreeable feeling. It's not in my stomach nor is it in my head. Then where? In my heart? What does the heart care about all these feelings? It keeps doing its job, beating away. Who has this disagreeable feeling? Is it me who has built a separate nest called the "I"? Who am I? What am I to myself? ... No use. Even before UG set his foot in Bangalore, Mahesh had warned me. Not just warned. He sounded a death knell on the phone, but I did not listen. "UG is going to see to your end, beware, my friend" – with words such as these he tried to prepare me as best as he could. I laughed within myself at Mahesh's foolishness. "What can UG do to someone who is ready to die? Could anyone do anything more horrible than that?" – I was so confident.

Then UG came to Bangalore and the fire in my heart was lit. My mind has not been at peace for all these ten days. Whenever UG came earlier, he would burn me with his words. So, this time I thought I should be careful and stay away. I decided that as much as possible I would try to avoid the situations where I might be left alone with him.

But this time, UG is not saying anything to me. And I am unable to bear his presence. Why? As much as I reassure myself, I cringe when I see UG, as if I am facing Yama, the God of Death, himself. My only thought is how to get away from him. My mind tries to run here and there finding some useless errands to do. If I force myself to sit in front of UG by "dragging myself by the ear", my mind complains as if it has gone crazy. It heckles loudly about UG before his words even come out of his mouth. "Why do you listen to this stuff? You have been listening to it all these years. How has it benefited you? Get up and get out!" it commands with authority. But where to go? And for how long?

Then, UG appears again. "My God, he came back so soon" – I beat my chest. "Why does he come here?" – my mind frowns. How many people from America to Hong Kong, how many types of people from various foreign countries, how many friends, pine day and night, all starving for UG's gaze, for a word from his mouth or for a smile? I list in my mind many of them by name (as far as I could remember). "You don't even appreciate the great fortune that has fallen on you! What a pity! You frown when the person who doesn't accept anyone's invitation comes right here to your door! Whom do you think he has come here for? For himself or his own pleasure?" This dumb mind doesn't respond. Still it frowns. It doesn't have the strength to refute my argument, but it doesn't quit its ploys to defeat me. "You crazy fellow, you fall into the confusion that it's all for your own good and set fire to your own house. You will be extinguished as you wait and watch; watch how that UG will drag you into perdition. He has already turned you into a useless fellow. He didn't leave you a penny of your earnings. What have you gained from his friendship? What interest in life did he let you keep? Where is your music? What happened to your literary taste? Where is your poet's heart hidden, my poor fellow, the heart which went into ecstasies watching the flowers, the birds, children, blue skies and stars that sparkled in the deep dark night? Look at yourself just once and observe how your being has been warped. You still want to sing to the tune of UG? Miserable fellow, listen to my advice; it's not too late. Take care of this craziness before it boils over from your heart into your throat and gets into your head from there," says my mind settling down in its seat. But why all this baseless hostility? Why can't I accept the situation even after I recognise all the help and caring UG has given my family and me? Then what do I really want? I don't understand that either. "Right now, I must escape from UG's clutches, that's all," my mind insists.

* * *

When Suguna started a conversation with Rajasekhara Reddi

the other night with just one question, "How is your book coming along?" all the sadness, frustration and despair that have been pent-up in him for years broke loose. For half an hour he spoke before UG how tightly his life has been tied to that book and how that book has squeezed him high and dry, rendering him impotent until it is finished.

"Not a single day passes without my lamenting, 'How did this UG happen to me? Why did I ever meet him? Why did that guy B.L. Narayana call me and introduce me to him in the first place?'" His book is titled *Jivana Lila*. Rajasekhar is trying to present UG's life in the form of a novel for the first time in Telugu literature. He has submitted it to the novel competition of TANA Association in the US. If they select the book, they will publish it as well as give him a cash prize of Rs.120, 000. "They haven't rejected the book; nor have they accepted and published it. That's the fact of the matter," Rajasekhar concluded.

* * *

Is *Sadhana* helpful?

Between 14 and 21 years of age, UG went through all possible travails to learn about the state of release. In 1932, the head of the Siva Ganga *Pitha* [*seat of religion*] initiated him by giving him the *Siva Mantra*. Since then he had been repeating the *mantra*. UG says he also used to repeat the *Gayatri Mantra* three thousand times a day. For seven years he practiced meditation, yoga, *pranayama* and such in Swami Sivananda's presence.

Even in those days, the experiences he had had were not ordinary. When he was 14, Master Kuthumi, whom Theosophists believe in, appeared to him. UG says that Kuthumi accompanied him in his subtle body for two years. How is that possible? UG says that our thoughts have so much power. It seems more appropriate to call them our "will" than our "thoughts". The power of the will is so immense. Whenever UG thought of him Master K.H. would appear before him. "Thought is very powerful. You can create your God in front of you; you can take a walk with Him hand in hand," he says now, meaning that the visions he had had in those days were all created by him. He says there was no end to his spiritual experiences. *Samadhi – savikalpa and nirvikalpa Samadhi* – happened to him easily. He experienced all sorts of states of bliss. "Is that all there is to those experiences? If I could experience them, then I must have had previous knowledge about them. I was imagining what I had already known and was deluded into thinking that I was experiencing something new," he concluded and brushed those experiences all aside.

Just as Nachiketa's strong urge to find out what death is brought him to the abode of Yama, the urge to know "What is that state called release; and what is that unequalled state which prophets like Buddha and Sankara proclaimed?" became a wildfire within UG and finally consumed his "garden of life". A thriving family, name and fame in society, inherited wealth – were all consumed like fuel in the fire of life. On his 49th birthday he himself was consumed in that fire as the last piece of firewood. What finally remained? Was the fire extinguished? Did he realise the truths he was seeking? "Nothing of the sort," declares UG, "That UG is gone; he has never returned. A fire which smoulders day and night, a fire covered with ashes, constantly burns silently just as rice husk that has caught fire. You can't see it from the outside. But if you touch it, it will burn you."

Venkata Chalapati insists that all the *sadhanas* UG had practiced before surely helped him. Not just Chalapati, but anyone who is caught in the nexus of cause and effect would assert the same. "The repetition of Siva *mantra* or the repetition of *Gayatri* – how can he claim that none of them was of any use? His present state is indeed the result of those *sadhanas*," they say, as if they know it all. They try to convince UG as if he has been caught in some confusion.

Many people strongly believe that there is no possibility of anything happening without a cause, although they don't believe that whatever they see, whatever appears to the senses or occurs to the mind is literally real. "We may not see the cause on the surface, but it must be there," they argue. When UG says to them, "This is purely acausal; none of the struggles I went through or the efforts I had made have any relevance to it," they smile with their eyes, as if they know what has happened. With statements like, "UG detests tradition and ancient ways. Although he admits that he followed them, he is reluctant to give them credit. That's why he puts them down," they justify their beliefs.

Is UG deliberately misleading us? Is he trying to hoodwink us with his tricky words?

"This occurrence is acausal" – he said this not just today; he has been saying it ever since the Calamity had occurred. In fact, it's probably not an exaggeration to say that UG is the only person who has been emphasising this from the beginning so clearly and consistently, without leaving any room for misconception.

Every event is independent. Our daily events are not connected to one another. "You" are the one who is linking them up and creating a cause-effect relationship. If you watch UG's daily conduct of life, this "linkless activity" becomes quite evident.

When we wake up every morning, how do we know that the "yesterday's we" is the same as "today's we"? Isn't it on the basis of memory? That means our whole existence is memory. There is nothing outside of memory. Based on it, we string together the various incidents that occur in our everyday life. If that string is broken, the events become scattered. It is this truth that UG strives to show us; no, it is the truth that he appears to us as striving to show.

Venkata Chalapati closed his eyes for a little while and fell into deep contemplation. He has one great trait: he is not keen on selling his beliefs.

Whether we agree or disagree with what UG says, we gain little. By merely learning that there is no cause-effect relationship in our day-to-day activities we will not be transformed into Gods. Even that knowing is part of the cause-effect relationship. This [*statement*] too is [*based on*] knowing. If we keep thinking like this, like peeling an onion layer by layer, we will have nothing left in our hands. But our tears from the fumes won't stop.

* * *

Swami Vidyanarayana Tirtha

There is a note in my notebook saying that Kuppuswami, a disciple of Swami Vidyanarayana Tirtha, requested the Swami to write a biography of UG. This probably happened when Swamiji visited UG in 1997. "My request is that you should write a book on UG. He is a kind of new species. Being a doctor yourself and also a saint, you are better equipped to write on the biological aspects of UG's "Calamity" or enlightenment. It will surely help the whole of mankind," said Kuppuswami. But it never happened. Swamiji by that time had already contemplated a prolonged travel.

There is a small twist here. This happened when Swami Vidyanarayana Tirtha visited UG on the Farm House. The day was May 3rd, 1997, Saturday. Swamiji arrived with four of his disciples from Rajajinagar around noon.

The things UG said that day: "The human species is the worst on this planet. If this species is wiped out, nothing is lost. I am discussing with the administrators of MIT about the possibility of creating a trust for a project to wipe out the human species. The legal adviser there asked me, 'Who will approve of such a project?'" Then UG talked about the pineal gland, the *ajna chakra*. "It takes over the control of the body. From then on all actions of the body are controlled by the pineal gland, not by thought."

"Nature discards the perfected model. Once it perfects a model, it discards it. It has no interest in reproducing or making copies of it."

"If you are lucky to touch life at a point where no one else has touched it, whatever is there begins to express itself."

"You make this [me] obsolete. It's not going to help anybody."

"There is no use in writing books or recording tapes."

"I am determined to destroy what I've said before. This is the last phase of my life..."

Swamiji said, "UG is the ultimate God. He stands for that. I am a nobody compared to him."

Swamiji continued: "Now you had the *darshan* of the Lord. In this world there are several groups. Some connected to Siva; some are the followers of Vishnu; some are the followers of Madhvacharya, and so on. But an *avatar* like UG comes rarely to show the true path."

UG replied to them: "You came to the wrong man."

Swamiji cast a mischievous look at UG. After a while he asked UG, "What are the Swiss people like? What is their characteristic nature?"

UG said: "All people are the same. Be they Indian, American, Swiss or Russian. Everybody is after one thing: happiness without a moment of unhappiness. Permanent happiness is what everybody is seeking. Unfortunately it doesn't exist anywhere. That's the tragedy of the human race."

Swamiji then said something to UG in Kannada that meant "You are elder to me in all respects." UG smiled and remarked in Kannada: "*Kannada barolla*" [*"I can't speak Kannada"*]. There was a burst of laughter from the gathering. Suddenly, UG's face became serious. He turned to Swamiji and said: "What do you want sir? You want all this and heaven too. Whatever you want you already know. How can you ask for a thing which you don't know? What I am saying is not in your field of knowing. You want to experience the oneness. You are already one with That. There is no separateness. That is what I am saying. Whatever you are doing is the one that is creating the separateness. It is strengthening that separateness."

Mohan interrupted and asked, "What shall we do, UG? Why can't you help us? You understand our situation very well. Can't you help us?"

"You don't need any help. I know that you don't want to accept that fact," said UG.

Mohan turned to Swamiji and asked, "Swamiji, do you have any question to ask UG?"

Swamiji smiled and said, "I have come here to enjoy his presence, not to bother him with questions."

Then he added as his advice to all that gathered, "Just listen, connect and leave."

* * *

Knowledge needs separation...

[*On May 3rd, 1997, Saturday, UG talked about logic and its usefulness in real life.*]

"When I was young I was repeating Annambhatta's book on logic, *Tarka Samgraha:* '*Yatra yatra dhumah, tatra tatra vahnih,*' wherever there is smoke, there is fire. That's the most absurd logic. I don't even say this is hard – [*UG touches the table*], that this is a chair. My touch doesn't tell me, my eyes don't tell me that this is a chair. I may be looking at it for a length of time, but I never tell myself that this is a chair. Hard! My foot doesn't tell that the touch is hard or that the bench is hard. I have necessarily to separate myself to know that the touch is hard. Thought has to step in and separate the two. Otherwise, there is no translation. You too don't know what you are looking at. You are all dead. What is there is something living. The dead structure in which you are operating can never capture that living thing. It burns. That's why I said to that scientist who wanted to tell me that there is no space, no time and all that. I listened to that crap; then I asked, 'Look here, buddy, do you mean to say there is no space? When you are about to fuck your wife, or bitch, or somebody, if there is no space as you say, can there be love-making? Can there be a wife, if there is no space?' That man was aghast. He held his head in both hands and said, 'Oh

God! I never thought of that! What can I do? How can I go on with my scientific pursuits?'"

* * *

He won't even forget a bunch of coriander...

That day, June 17, 1997, UG was in Bangalore, upstairs in "Hridaya Vihar". It was 6 a.m. in the morning. UG was sitting on the swing in the balcony. The neem tree next to him was whisking away with new foliage. The summer weather in Bangalore was pleasant. I came upstairs carrying a tray of oatmeal and cream for UG. He took the tray and placed it next to him on the swing. Major and I sat in the rattan chairs facing him. "The weather is very good. The cool breeze is pleasant," remarked UG. "The wind is blowing me away. I have no consciousness that the body is moving;" he said again, "there is no one here. I wonder how the words are coming out of me." Just then, the Australians called on the phone. UG's birthday was still ahead. "Mere greetings are of no use! They should be backed with lots of money!" UG told them.

There was a scarcity of coriander in the market place. You couldn't find it anywhere. Suguna sent some people out on a mission of a coriander hunt. UG must have observed all this. In the evening we all went to Gandhi Bazaar to buy something in the Food World Store. By then we had all but forgotten about coriander. As soon as he got out of the car, UG said to Suguna, "Look, they are selling coriander there." We were all surprised that UG remembered. "This is a computer machine. The fact that it's hard to find coriander was registered in it. Without any prompting, it noticed the coriander," said UG.

* * *

"Go to your president and beg him..."

A day in June 1997. We went with UG to the Commercial Street. UG said he wanted to buy a tracksuit. At the beginning of the street a well-dressed stranger stopped UG and started talking to him. I thought he knew UG. I walked closer toward them. He was asking UG to help him with money – a stylish beggar. He was not happy with pennies. He wanted rupees. I was watching with curiosity to see how UG would respond or how much he would give him. "Go to your President Shankar Dayal Sharma and beg him. Don't ask me," he said and moved away fast. The stylish beggar's face turned pale. I followed UG quickly.

* * *

Gangayya

This is an incident from UG's youth. When he was studying in Gudiwada, he employed a Harijan boy called Gangayya as his secretary. Gangayya used to do all the chores and ride a bicycle with UG on its back seat. When UG's grandmother wanted to ask UG about anything, she would have to ask his secretary. "How many days will the boy stay? When will he leave?" she would ask and learn about his plans. Gangayya was quite intelligent. He used to compose poetry ex tempore in Telugu. In later years, he passed the IAS Examinations and became a government official. Apparently, years later, he met UG in Delhi and invited him to his home. UG realised that the official was totally corrupt. He was earning a lot of money. "What did you do for your folks and people of your caste? You have such a high status now. Have you helped them in any way?" asked UG. Gangayya replied that he couldn't do anything. "I have two daughters. I must marry them and see to it that they will live happily. That's why I'm going through all this trouble," he said.

* * *

"You want me to help you die?"

In the book *Mystique of Enlightenment* there is a chapter with the same title. It was James Brodsky who selected and transcribed all those paragraphs from the tapes of UG's conversations. Back then he had been a full male. Now he has changed his sex and became Jane. She is close to Julie. Before he had met UG, James had talked with JK for two hours about his urges to commit suicide. JK tried to prevent him from committing suicide in many ways. Later, when he finally met UG, he mentioned his problem to him. UG encouraged his suicide attempts and his urge to commit suicide by asking him, "Do you want some help from me to die?" With that James' sickness had disappeared. He never contemplated suicide again.

* * *

"Humans should reduce themselves to the level of animals..."

On June 26, 1997, G. S. Mani, the famous Karnatic musician arrived in Bangalore from Madras by the Mail train. He came especially to meet UG. He spent the whole day with UG and left the same night. "Humans should reduce themselves to the level of animals in all their activities. That's the only way the human race can survive," said UG in the course of his conversations with Madurai G.S. Mani.

"Which is superior – the human race or other animal species?" I asked UG. "That question is still based on the assumption that human birth is a rare privilege. Actually, there is no higher or lower," said UG.

* * *

"Your relationship with your money says it all..."

Once, Vedantam Satyanarayana (in the same year, i.e., 1997) came to see UG. He was about to make a remark by saying, "Every time we come to you...." UG interrupted him and said, "You are wasting your time and money." Vedantam was taken aback. "No, that's not what I meant. What I was trying to say was that each time we meet you, you are evaluating our spiritual progress," said Vedantam.

"Your relationship with your money says it all. Even if you give away your money in charity, it doesn't mean anything. It's the same as hoarding it. One has to see for himself or herself how one is related to money," said UG.

* * *

"I have yet to see a person who does things without expecting anything in return," said UG.

"What about yourself, sir?" asked Vedantam. "I am not doing anything. I am not giving to others anything that I want," replied UG.

* * *

Part III

"You Have Come to the Wrong Man"

His name was Chakravarti Anantachar. As his name indicates, he was born in a Vaishnava family which followed the tradition of Vishishtadvaita [*qualified nondualism*] taught by Sri Ramanujacharya. Although Mr. Anantachar was a profound scholar in Sanskrit grammar and logic and an authority on Ramanujacharya's philosophy, he was also a great admirer of Sankara and his Advaita philosophy. His lectures on Sankara's Advaita Vedanta always drew large crowds and earned him a good standing in the spiritual circles of Bangalore. That is how several of my friends got to know of him. Once upon a time, my friend Krishnamurthy was very close to him and was attending his lectures almost every day.

One day in June 1998, our friend Venkata Chalapati spoke about UG to Anantachar describing UG as a "Jivanmukta". Anantachar was impressed and expressed his interest in meeting UG. But UG dissuaded Venkata Chalapati: "Why do you want to bring him? You say that he is a scholar and a professional speaker. Such people have an investment in the tradition they believe in. How can he listen to me?" But Venkata Chalapati's eagerness prevailed.

At last, on Sunday June 21 1998, Anantachar walked into Major's Farm House to meet UG. He was accompanied by Venkata Chalapati and Krishnamurthy.

UG respectfully offered a seat next to him on the sofa. Some of us sat on the floor and some on the available chairs. I wrote down the points of discussion between UG and Anantachar. Here is the text of the conversation that took place on that bright sunny afternoon.

Anantachar introduced himself as a theoretical Vedanta exponent, and a mere speaker and scholar on matters of Vedanta. He started his conversation with UG saying, "Those who are in the highest spiritual state are said to be in possession of several powers."

UG made no comment.

Anantachar: Don't you think that through meditation one can achieve great heights in spiritual life?

UG: Meditation should not be given any importance at all. That's my feeling.

Anantachar: Then what shall we do?

UG: Nothing; do nothing.

Anantachar: [Smiling] In that case everyone becomes a yogi.

UG: I am not a yogi.

Anantachar: But you are a yogi.

He then looked at the people sitting around. The problem was he hadn't read any of UG's books before he came to see him. He was not familiar with UG's point of view. So, he was visibly perturbed by UG's statements. After a while, he confessed he was not able to follow what UG was trying to communicate.

Anantachar: Anyway sir, you are a widely travelled person. Don't you think it is possible to bring out a universal philosophy to end all conflicts?

UG: Universal philosophy as such doesn't exist except as an idea. That goal has created the actual problem.

Anantachar: Do you mean to say that a universal life doesn't exist? All the masters of all religions talked of the oneness of life.

UG: You are an expression of that life. The mosquito that is sucking your blood is another expression of that life. The garden slug out there is another expression. The problem is we want to understand life. We try to understand. That attempt is bound to create conflict.

Anantachar: Advaita Vedanta talks about that life as anirvacaniya, indefinable.

UG: In that case, why should they talk about it? [Now UG's tone got sharper.] If there is anything as the "beyond", it can never be captured, contained or given expression to. How can they describe it as bliss, beatitude and all that nonsense? If they know that it is anirvacaniya, they should have stopped right there.

Anantachar: As philosophers they wanted to postulate...

UG: What good is that to you sir? Philosophers as I know are lovers of wisdom. That's what they are. Philosophy only helps to sharpen the intellect.

Anantachar: Sir, how to determine whether a man is wise or not?

UG: You have no way of knowing.

Anantachar: Sankara describes the characteristics of an enlightened man. Even in the Gita it is said...

UG: They are all empty words and empty phrases, sir! They mean nothing. What's the use of all those words? They haven't helped you. You are still asking the same question.

Everybody laughs. Anantachar is visibly shaken. He asks for a cup of water and empties two cups, one after the other.

Anantachar: We have to use words to communicate with each other.

UG: I say and maintain that no communication is possible and none is necessary.

Anantachar: But we have no other way to wisdom.

UG: Why are we not ready to accept that "wisdom" is a real block?

Anantachar looks at the people around helplessly. He turns to Venkata Chalapati and says "I can't understand what he is saying." He then turns to UG:

Anantachar: You have gone a little above my head. I am not able to follow you. I have worked for several years academically...

UG: But I am an illiterate...

Anantachar: No. No. I can't agree. You are an enlightened person. Only to a few are gifted to be enlightened. An enlightened person is above everything. In my opinion, when a man forgets all his surroundings in the contemplation of the undivided Self, that state, according to Sankara, is the "Brahmi State". My practice of meditation is very poor. I haven't done any sadhana. But I want to. I am only a Jnanamargi.

UG: I am not a scholar like you. But I studied Advaita philosophy. Prof. Mahadevan was our teacher of Advaita philosophy.

Anantachar: Sir, how can we understand the world?

UG: There is no need to understand the world.

Anantachar: Otherwise, how can we be in contact with the world?

UG: Do you think you are really in contact with anything? Do you think you are looking at that man? Do you think you have ever looked at your wife even once? If you once looked at your wife, that would be the end of the whole relationship. You look at everything through the knowledge you have. It's the knowledge about the things around that creates the world for you. You cannot experience anything that you do not know. In that sense I say and maintain that there is no such thing as a new experience at all. How can you have contact with the world?

Anantachar: As long as we breathe and live in this world we keep the contact.

UG: No, on no level can you contact anything.

Anantachar was disturbed with the rise in UG's voice. He became fidgety in his seat next to UG. He asked for more water and Mohan gives him some.

Mohan: [to Anantachar] Do you accept what he is saying, sir?

UG: How can he say anything? He is not in a position to say.

Anantachar started quoting the Mandukya Upanishad. "There is Para wisdom and there is Apara wisdom. When once you renounce Vritti Gnana, then Swarupa Jnana dawns on you. Ultimately, *upasantoyam atma*, as the instruction in the Mandukya indicates."

At this point, UG suddenly flared up. He burst out saying that Mandukya Upanishad does not even have as much worth as toilet paper. He called Sankara a bastard for writing commentaries on Upanishads. He started his tirade on Gowdapada for writing the karika to Mandukya and called him also a bastard.

This was too much for Anantachar. He started trembling with anger. He could no longer sit in a composed manner. Mohan was trying to calm him down handing him more cups of water. "Drink more water sir, and sit comfortably," Mohan told him.

Anantachar: [In an agitated voice, looking at the people around] This is too much, sir, He uses such uncivilised terminology. How can he call Sankara a bastard? How can an enlightened person use such foul language?

Then UG again flared up.

UG: Yes, I shall maintain Sankara was a bastard! Mandukya is shit! It is his shit that is coming out of your mouth. What do you have to say? That is my question. Don't repeat Sankara, Gowdapada and all that nonsense. You are just repeating. A tape recorder does a better job than you. What you say, does it operate in your life? You can teach fools from the platform and make a living. I have no objection. But it has not touched you. How can anybody describe that state as love and bliss? Love divides and separates. There is already division. How can there be love?

Anantachar stood up. He couldn't take it anymore. He said, "I came here hoping to see an enlightened person. I never expected I would be meeting such a negative person instead."

UG countered immediately saying "You came to the wrong man. You can go now."

Anantachar folded his hands as a mark of respect and walked out of the room.

* * *

The Story of Sharmila

February 25, 1999, Thursday -- Hyderabad

At Rajasekhar's home. I sit at the dining table writing. Above me the ceiling fan is spinning. It's 7:30 a.m. Prabhakar, Raja and I chatted last night till 11:30 and then went to bed. Last evening, Gopi brought me here from Venkatapuram on his motorcycle. We arrived at Amirpeta at 4:30 p.m. We didn't know that we were about to be acquainted with a great person a few minutes later. Raja had written to me about her in his letters. When I read his letter to UG in Palm Springs, I learned some new things.

Before I left on my journey for Palm Springs, Bharati phoned to tell me, "An anonymous disciple has been pining to see UG. She is not an ordinary woman. She is rich in every way. Tell me when UG is coming. He must come and meet her."

"Such a wealthy lady could call UG and talk to him. Why should UG call her?" I replied.

"She won't call. Tell him that I asked him to," she said.

I conveyed what she said to UG. Then he said immediately, "Perhaps that unknown disciple is this lady whom Rajasekhar has been describing." Yesterday, that suspicion has been confirmed. This is the lady who has been worshipping UG, reading his books all these years without yet meeting him and trying to understand UG's trend of thought and implement it constantly in her everyday life. I thought that perhaps this might be the God-sent lady who has been prophesied by the astrologer friends of UG as the unique lady who has been waiting for the favour of the planets like a cuckoo bird to surely step into UG's life.

Yesterday afternoon, exactly at 5 p.m., Sharmila stepped into Raja's living room. She wore a green sari with an apple-coloured border. She was neither tall nor short but chubby and simple. She had attractive eyes and a beautiful face. She was probably a bit older than 40 years, but she looked younger. There was great peace and contentment in her eyes. In her demeanour she manifested an unperturbed nature.

* * *

I move from the dining table to the sofa in the living room and continue writing. After Raja's mother has passed away, the room has been transformed. How worried she was about what would become of her son after she was gone! Now, Raja has a new life. A new enthusiasm runs through his life. He has gotten the whole house painted and repairs made; the house got a facelift. He decorated the house like a museum with the help of Kirti, his daughter. He hung beautiful pictures on the walls. In this room he has pictures of all the great people; Amma of Jillellamudi, Jiddu Krishnamurti, Aurobindo, Mother, Bhagavan Ramana Maharshi, UG and Shirdi Sai Baba greet you kindly from the walls. In the corners you see brass lamp posts, metal statues of Gods -- a statue of Nataraja and a Lingam of Siva with *Nandi*, the bull. A white statue of Ganesha seated comfortably. Besides these, there is an art piece from Tanjore – apparently Sharmila had presented it to him. There is a wool carpet on the floor and a nice sofa set. You can see a big round pillow and other pillows there for back support. These and many other things give the room a look of high status. In the middle of the room there is a small table. On it is a glass slab, and on the slab is placed a brass bowl with *pan* paraphernalia. There is a box in the middle of the bowl with imbedded shells. In a corner, there are a couple of brass decorative plates. The display in the room reveals Rajasekhar's artistic temperament. A calm that transcends the artwork seems to pervade the room. Raja has been using this as his worship room. There is incense burning and the room is filled with the fragrance of joss sticks. There is no scope for any other fumes to rise except the fragrances of flowers. Gopi too was greatly impressed by this room.

* * *

The "i" in the name "Sharmila" is elongated. You should pronounce the name as "Sharmeelaa". We thought that the name was perhaps Muslim. I told people in Palm Springs that her name was Sharmila. She now said that her name "Sharmila" is a symbol for "Hrim" *Bijakshara*. She studied in a medical college in Calcutta. Perhaps she had changed her name there.

First of all, who is this lady? How was she attracted to UG? What about this crazy worship of UG even before she had ever met him? Such questions naturally occur to anyone. I asked her in person, "Tell us about your background, how you came to be interested in UG and such other details." She replied, "Oh, even if I tell about it every day, a whole year will not be enough," and laughed. When she talks you feel like you want to keep listening to her. She doesn't have to struggle to find the right word nor does she have difficulty in translating her thoughts into words. I thought she showed an ability to speak on a public platform, in meetings or assemblies, like an expert, fluently and profoundly. She seemed to be naturally endowed with the facility to speak and express her ideas clearly. We listened to her words spellbound.

About five years ago she was introduced to UG when she had read Mahesh Bhatt's biography of UG in English. She doesn't agree with the account UG gives of his natural state, saying that it's only of contemporary value and will not be of use to future generations. On the basis of the information in that book, it became clear to her that UG is an impersonal individual and that a universal consciousness is manifested in him. She said:

This is no ordinary matter. From the beginning of creation, many teachers and great people have pledged their lives to the grace of God and to realising the Self; they did many *sadhanas* and had extraordinary experiences. Some became the crest jewels of mankind. People today are paying homage to them. But it's different with UG. Mother Creation tried out many models. None of the models could understand her sorrow. All the *avatars* who have descended on mankind, the prophets who have appeared and the supreme teachers who have spread their messages have only helped to break up the human race into pieces. They strove to divide humanity into religions and planted the seeds of that poison. Even if they didn't preach it themselves, their teachings have had such a consequence. However, for the first time, Mother Creation found UG's model. This model strove to erase completely the consciousness in himself that he is a separate individual. There is only one courageous model who is prepared to be completely merged in this universal consciousness without keeping even a trace of himself and who is prepared to be consumed like fuel in the fatal fire of life. Exactly after 2,500 years, Mother Creation found a model which is on a par with Tathagata [*Buddha*]. Before UG, she had hopes in the models of Ramana Maharshi, Jiddu Krishnamurti and Aurobindo. But no such models could satisfy Mother Creation. All her hopes were dashed.

At last, when the model of UG sat on the bench under a tree in Switzerland exactly on his 49th birthday, the labour pains of Mother Earth had begun. The heavens held their breath. The seven mountains and seven valleys looked into their depths and stood still. With one stroke Creation became paralysed with the scream of Mother Earth. For one moment, there were tremors in UG's body. All the nine *nadis* and six *chakras* whirled around. For one moment, the whole of Creation was in disarray. Heavens shook hands with the underworld. The mountain peaks kissed their own shadows. The next moment everything settled down. The windstorm that shook the directions calmed down. In the model sitting on the bench, the universal consciousness shaped itself as a newborn child. That was a true new birth. It was a new birth for the human kind. It was a unique experience unheard of before in history.

That's what Sharmila had noticed. That's why she is so interested in UG. She is infinitely fond of this 'model' called UG. She says, "His is an impersonal self." She says, "The time has come for the 'model' to spread throughout the world."

There is no individual in UG; only the collective. In him, there is no tradition of any country. In him is hidden the evolution of the whole human race. Evolution in all its stages made room for itself there. To say it in other words, there is nothing. Everything is washed away and there is a hollow like in a reed flute. In it, the winds of universal consciousness resonates the seven notes.

Sharmila makes this truth clear. If she could explain this to Bharati and Aparajita and get them interested in it, I must congratulate her.

Sharmila doesn't talk much about herself. "I am always in the wakeful-sleep state," she said once. I haven't met any person, except UG, who could say that. I was stunned. It's not that she didn't know the meaning of those words. She has had many divine visions. It's evident from her appearance that she is a holy person who has attained heights of spirituality. She says she is Raja's "sister". She gives him gifts. She is wealthy. Yesterday she gave me a silver engraving of Lakshmi. She says, "Keep it, it will do you good." The question "Why?" remained in my mind.

Sharmila -ii

It's almost 10 o'clock, time for Sharmila's arrival. The dishes Raja had made last night, the tomato chutney Sharmila had brought and the *idlis* Raja has served today are sitting still in my stomach. I didn't believe that I could sit in this room and write like this. I am not sorry that Mr. Raju has not come. Yesterday, Sharmila had borrowed my yet-to-be-published book to get it copied. Raja told me that her husband is a professor.

Sharmila has a great interest in spiritual pursuits. She has read the books of Andrew Cohen and Aurobindo; and it seems that she has a coterie of disciples. Apparently, they gather around her, listen to her messages and record them. As she was saying goodbye yesterday, she handed a small photo of herself to me and said, "Please show this to UG and after he looks at it, you please burn it. I don't know if I will be fortunate enough to see him or not." When I asked Raja "why can't she come to Bangalore," he told me that circumstances wouldn't permit it. Will UG ever come to Hyderabad? Who knows if he will?

* * *

All those who studied UG's horoscope have said with confidence that a unique lady will enter his life. That should have happened by now. Who is that woman? Could it be Sharmila? I think she is a multi-millionaire. She is the mother of two girls. That she can afford to distribute properties worth 40 million rupees to each of her daughters shows that her husband is a multi-millionaire. But when you see her, she doesn't look like she is wealthy. She looks simple. By profession she is a medical doctor. Later she also took up the job of teaching arts and crafts to children; and started a "finishing school" with 30 different subjects for women and the destitute. She said she has recently closed down the institution that she had run for fifteen years. She is an adept in 30 different crafts; and she has a great appreciation for art. She is cultured and lives a righteous life. She is a treasure house of all the noble qualities. Such a person has surfaced after such a long time. She gives comfort to Bharati and prepares her for her father's grace. It's clear that the unimaginable change in Bharati's attitude towards her father is due to Sharmila's influence.

March 1, 1999

Morning 5:25 a.m. The city is still asleep. I felt as if I was awake all the time.

For a while I might have dozed off. Then I woke up soon after. I first woke up at 4:30 a.m. But by the time I got up from bed it was 5:15 a.m. I spent almost all of yesterday with Venkata Chalapati and Dakshinamurti. I related to both of them the news of Hyderabad, at least the highlights of it, if not all the details.

I don't know what I have already written about Sharmila. Saturday, the day I was leaving, she spent from 1:30 p.m. in the afternoon till 6 p.m. chatting with us. The more I watched her and the more I learned about her, the more she seemed like an extraordinary woman.

After meeting me, she gave a testimonial about me, as much as her intuitions had indicated to her. Apparently, she had observed cosmic rays falling over my head. "There is a great positive force in Mr. Chandrasekhar," she told Raja. But when I look into myself, I can find nothing but holes and ditches. Anyway, whatever I think about myself is only a product of my imagination. If I am myself a fiction, can all the things I experience and learn on the basis of it be real? What, indeed, is real? Is there anything true or eternal? If there is such a thing, there is no scope for me to find it. Anything that I happen to grasp with this tiny narrow personality cannot be real. How can I know even that?

Sharmila-iii

UG must have left Sydney and arrived in Stapleton. I must phone him and find out when he is coming here. His Australian friends hold him dearer than their own lives, especially Jeffrey. I think Jeffrey has some extrasensory powers. Sharmila is also endowed with such powers.

"Are you experiencing summer heat in the body?" I asked her as I was saying goodbye.

"I asked you because I feel that if you include *mung dahl* in your diet, you will have less heat during summer," I explained.

"I live in my body at the cellular level, united with the cells; so nothing bothers me. At the peak of summer a cold wave starts from inside my body; so, the common bodily changes that happen to everyone don't touch me," she said to reassure me. Then I quoted UG's words about food saying that the body can manufacture all the nutrients it needs from sawdust. She remarked, "That's absolutely true; but only for him; not for all bodies. As a result of the changes that took place in his body, the Mother of Creation prepared such a body for him."

It would be interesting to mention here Sharmila's explanation of how the body is a mixture of the five elements and how it obtains its energy:

Three quarters of the globe of earth is covered by water and only a quarter of its surface is earth. Many times vaster than water is fire or light. Larger than that is air or atmosphere. Above that is the sky or space. In this hierarchy, each is lighter than the one below it. There is so much difference between the most solid, dense earth and the sky or space. The earth, water, light, air and space – each of the five elements is lighter and thinner than the previous one. Each is more extended than the previous one. It's possible to derive energy from each of them. You can sustain life by just breathing air. The body can live on sunlight alone. It's possible.

"So," she concludes, "the less you consume solid substances, the easier it is to support the body. "

* * *

[Post Script: During March, 2001, Sharmila came to Bangalore with Bharati and met UG. But after that brief visit she just drifted away even from her friends; let alone her acquaintances. I tried in vain to get in touch with her through my friend Rajasekhar, in the meantime. Suddenly on November 7, 2009, Sharmila showed up at our home in Bangalore. She stayed for one day with us. "My life was never the same after my meeting with UG" said Sharmila recounting the events that led to her walking out of the family and leading a forlorn life in Hyderabad. On December 1, 2009, Suguna and I happened to visit Sharmila in her abode. A small room in the basement of an apartment building in the heart of Hyderabad city is her home now. She rarely meets people and spends most of her time in communion with her Devi and other spiritual masters who adorn the walls of her simple dwelling. Occasionally, she is dragged into "Satsangs" by her loyal admirers.]

"My photograph is more powerful than me..."

March 10, 1999, Wednesday

Early this morning, I took oats, pineapple juice and cream upstairs for UG. UG and Major were on the balcony. UG eats his oatmeal by 6 a.m., swinging gently on the swing and chatting. We too chat away, sitting on the chairs before him and drinking coffee.

In the morning at 10 a.m., we went to the bank with UG. We finished all the deposit business, visited the tailor, Shankar, and then returned home in Major's car. At 11:45 a.m. Venkata Chalapati brought his car with the driver. We all went in both cars to the Farm House, spent half-an-hour there and returned at 1:45 p.m. The Malladis and Suguna also came with us. UG certified to Major that everything in the Farm House is in order.

Now I remember an important thing. Once upon a time, Major harboured an ambition of touring abroad, particularly of visiting the U.S. But after his wife passed away, as he got more and more acquainted closely with a variety of foreign faces through UG, his desire to visit all those countries had diminished. The more UG extolled their culture, the more he felt repelled by it. He resolved, "This is our country. And there is no way of life better than ours.

What's the point of going there?" No matter how many times UG prodded him, he brushed him off saying, "Please let me be as I am. I don't have any desire to visit those countries and see those spectacles."

Recently, after Christmas, on December 27, I called Major on the phone from Palm Springs and talked to him: "You must get a visa and leave for the U.S. right away. You must come." What I said raised a storm in his mind. I told him this earlier also, looking at his horoscope, that it was inevitable that he would travel to foreign lands. "Even if you don't like it, at the beginning of the Rahu stage, you're bound to travel." But getting a visa, buying a ticket and travelling abroad – these are all tasks that are beyond him. He complains and asks why he should be dragged into the street when he is living happily in this cottage, amidst this garden, alone, in the lap of nature, without a worry.

But what should he do about the current anxiety in his mind? He couldn't take the agitation anymore and sat looking at one of UG's photograph. Normally, he never looks at UG's photo; he doesn't pay any attention to it. Only when he has such problems that go over his head, he pours out his worries before UG. "He is asking me to come, UG. But I don't like to go. What do you want me to do? Should I tell him OK? Or should I say I won't go?" Thus he silently appealed to UG. A message from inside told him to say, yes. As soon as he said to himself "OK, as you please," all the chaos in his mind had calmed down. All his anxiety was removed as if it was erased clean from his mind. He narrated that story to UG and us yesterday at the breakfast table. UG made him repeat it to everyone over and over again.

UG's photo has greater power than UG. It performs wonders. I told those that gathered that there is no count of how many people have photos of UG protecting them in different ways.

* * *

UG told us another story confirming this: "My photograph is more powerful than me. Once, Robert was taking me around in

Amsterdam in his car. No matter how much he searched, he couldn't find a parking place. He had a UG photo on his dashboard. Normally he would be able to get a parking space without much difficulty as soon as he prayed to the photo. But this time, he couldn't find one, even though I was by his side. Finally, I told him, 'Drop me off here and then ask my photo; you will find the place.' And the moment I got out of the car, Robert found a parking space."

UG's drawing attention to the power of his own photo pleased me. Even UG doesn't know in how many ways and to how many people it has given comfort and still does.

* * *

March 11, 1999

Yesterday Yadunath brought an artist from "Prabhat Kalavidaru". The artist wished to demonstrate to UG the Bhagavad Gita in the form of a play. He said he would arrange for a stage in an auditorium and let us know by the end of the month. He said to me, "On that stage UG must speak about Bhagavad Gita." I didn't know how to reply to him. Yadunath himself admitted after a little while, "UG doesn't care about such things. He won't be happy." I told UG about it that night. Major burst out into laughter and commented "What! UG speak about Bhagavad Gita? After listening to him, who will remain in the auditorium?" and continued with his laughter. "Want to bet? I can give a talk on the Bhagavad Gita and please everyone present. How much will you bet?" challenged UG smiling. "Well, show us first, then we will believe you," Major concluded. With that the discussion stopped.

* * *

An Attempt to Strangle UG

– Aparajita

March 12, 1999

Yesterday, driving to the Farm House, Aparajita sat with Suguna in the car with UG. Apparently, UG had been attacking JK during the entire ride. As soon as they arrived at the Farm House, UG smiled and asked me and Suguna, "Why did you let this girl sit with me?" And picking on Aparajita, he said, "You couldn't seduce JK. You're so inept." She got all fired up. She couldn't stand that UG was making fun of her in front of everyone. UG got out of the car and sat in the living room. Aparajita sat next to him nestled in a rattan chair. "Why do you talk like that? Could people like you speak like that?" she admonished UG. UG, on his part, continued to use obscene language. Aparajita couldn't take it anymore. This belittling of JK and of her, especially by someone like UG -- how long could this jocularity go on? She suddenly leapt up and not stopping even when UG was trying to move away, she held him by her hands and squeezed his throat. All of us who had been watching this scene couldn't keep from laughing. She tried to strangle him two or three times. But eventually she calmed down by herself. That was some fun for UG. He is used to picking on her, teasing her and making her angry. She is now the Secretary of the JK Centre. "If they learn that you tried to strangle me, the JK gang will praise you," said UG making even more fun of her. We all enjoyed Aparajita's assault.

* * *

I must write about Radhakishan's story. He was very ill six months ago. When I phoned him some time back, he said he was just recovering. He had some intestinal infection with diarrhoea and vomiting, which could not be controlled. He was bedridden for some months. He suffered from bedsores for some more time. He was worried at that time that he might die. But he resolved in himself strongly that "I won't accept death until I see UG." Then he started recovering slowly. Now, this is the first time that he has seen UG since his illness. As soon as he set his eyes on him UG said, "You're the only one whom I have been thinking about, sir!" That moved me. I felt that it was Radhakishan's prayer, his longing to see UG that had brought UG here this time. Radhakishan is still able to come on his scooter. He passed all his assets and property on to his relatives. He has washed his hands off them and is now sitting, comfortably waiting for his final departure.

* * *

"I met a man..."

It was 2 p.m. in the afternoon. We had all returned to the Farm House at 1 p.m. in Venkata Chalapati's car after we had lunch. A Californian called Sky is now part of the Sai Baba group. He called on the phone from Whitefield and asked if he could come and see UG. He couldn't find UG's books. He left word with Suguna to ask me to bring some books to the Farm House. "Did you bring any books?" he asked me. I didn't bring any with me. I told him I would get them the next day. "Then I'll come tomorrow," he replied. "Why don't you come and meet the man? Is that not more important than the book?" I asked him. He laughed. "Okay, I will come right away," he said and, just as he promised, he came in an auto. After that, UG's talk turned out to be very interesting. Perhaps it was all intended for him. Jitendra Baba was sitting next to UG in a chair. UG spoke about many things. Sri Ramakrishna seemed to be influencing UG. UG was using the term "fuck" frequently, enunciating it clearly with his whole mouth. He mentioned Clinton's contention that oral sex is not a sin and said that Clinton quoted the Bible to support his claim. "You don't fuck the face anyway," he laughs. He reported that Ramakrishna used to pester the people who came to see him by asking them, "How much money do you have? How much will you give me?" Then he declared that Sri Ramakrishna was a homosexual.

Aside, Sky had been whispering in my ear, "How does UG know all these things?" "Those are all facts that came out in the newspapers or books which he had read," I answered. He asked UG, "What's your opinion of Nisargadatta?" UG narrated the story of his meeting with Nisargadatta. UG and Maurice Friedman were friends. Friedman was part of the JK gang at that time. It was in the days after the "Calamity" that Friedman met UG. An account of Friedman's mentioning about his meeting UG to Nisargadatta and what Nisargadatta said about UG have been printed in the 71st Chapter of *I am That*. After hearing about UG's unique experiences and the description of his natural state, Nisargadatta even predicted, "Your friend is talking now. But soon he will stop talking and remain silent." Later, Friedman cleverly arranged a meeting between UG and Nisargadatta in his house. He told UG that his daughter was sick and that she was hoping to see him; he invited him to his house. Thus, he arranged things so that UG could meet Nisargadatta. The two were together for about an hour. "I spoke in English and he in Marathi. Someone else who didn't know either of the languages very well translated us to each other. That's all that happened. Finally, when Friedman asked me what I thought about Nisargadatta, I replied, "I met a man," says UG. That's all that happened. But who knows what the inner meaning of it all is?

* * *

After Mohan arrived, the scene became quite interesting. Mohan interrupts UG with his questions. He doesn't care even if UG scolds him, shoos him away or abuses him in front of everyone; he just never quits questioning UG.

"Why do you come here? You won't get anything here. Why do you leave your office and hang around here?" asks UG "What can I do UG? I can't change. When you've come so many thousands of miles, what's the sense if I can't travel these few miles? Even if I sit in the office, I only think of you. I can't work. So, it's better to sit here than stay there," is Mohan's answer.

Then UG kept on talking till 5 p.m. Bob was videotaping quite a bit of it. I must have a look at it. UG's jabs at J.K. and talks about his encounters with J.K., his meeting with Ramana Maharshi and about his one-night stand. He talked about how with that single night's experience, not only his sex desire but the whole pleasure movement had burned out. In answer to one of Mohan's questions, he said, "When you can fuck your mother, your daughter or your sister, only then this is possible." I can't remember Mohan's exact question. That means, in order for duality to disappear and for you to be able to step into a reality devoid of space and time, you must be able to do such a thing. "Once you have sex – just sex without any ideas – you are finished," he says. It's dangerous to consider this as a method. UG never makes such a mistake. The Tantrics make sex as part of their *sadhana*. That's why he spurns it.

He talked about cancer, of his son Vasant dying of cancer, and of his advise to his son's girlfriend "forget about Vasant, find some other young man and be happy," on the very same day that Vasant died. Although the girl was furious at UG's advice, she did exactly what UG had suggested before the end of a year.

* * *

UG talks so intensely, for so many hours, using all his energy – it is amazing how he can talk like that. The food he eats is so little. He doesn't rest. [*Listening to him,*] everyone's eyes become heavy with drowsiness. The listeners feel that their throats are so parched that they feel they should go and get a drink of water. UG doesn't even ask for a glass of water. He talks ceaselessly about something or other. Where does he get so much energy? Yet, his body seems only a bit better than a cage of bones. There is an indescribable light in his face. His sharp eyes observe every movement.

"Recognition is UG. As soon as there is recognition, UG is present. Then he goes. Then there is another thing," when UG talks like that my head gets hot. I have only a vague understanding of what he is talking about; that's all. I don't understand. "You shouldn't understand. If you understand, you will not come to me; nor will you go to anyone else for help," says UG. The more you observe it, the more UG's tremendous energy dazzles you.

"Bob, I want you three to do something with the stuff Chandrasekhar has gathered," he said referring to Bob, Julie and me. As soon as he said, "I shall even ask Julie to come over here, if you three will do something with those archives," Bob and I shook hands. What should we do with the archives? Whatever we do, we must convert those tapes into VCDs or CDs before they deteriorate.

* * *

A One-Night Stand

March 14, 1999, Sunday

It is exactly a week since UG has arrived in this country. A week ago, I was involved in the arrangements for the School's anniversary celebrations. Bhagavan [*Sri Ramana Maharshi*] taught us that we must move as that Force moves us. That Force is within me, within my heart. If I can see it there, I can see its presence everywhere. That's the truth. But who is this who is pining to gain a vision of it? Am I something different from that Force? Every action, every thought and every experience is an attempt to multiply the pleasure-seeking a thousand times, says UG. God is the most extreme pleasure. The yearning is to gain the presence of God. UG explained this in many ways yesterday. He calls it the "pleasure movement". Long ago, he had realised clearly that every effort of his was prompted by that.

Venkata Chalapati said to UG yesterday:

You tell everyone that what one needs in life are just the two "F"s. You advise that we should double their quotas for the smoker and the drinker. Although you suggest that it's futile to suppress the desire for pleasure and that one should nurture them to the limits, what I observed in myself and everyone else is that those desires for pleasure won't satisfy us in the long run. Everyone will sometime or the other strongly want to become free from these pleasures and will retreat from them. Indeed, he wouldn't want to dedicate the rest of his life to those pleasures.

Then UG replied immediately, "To put that truth into practice doesn't depend on time. Realising that is not done by learning slowly, little bits at a time -- it must become clear instantly like a flash of lightning." He gave the example of Mahesh. In the past, Mahesh was an alcoholic; he drank liquor every night. He could not do without it. Once, when he came to Bangalore and was in pain because he couldn't buy a bottle of liquor, UG procured a bottle of Black Label through Brahmachari and gave it to him. He said:

I never condemned him by saying that he shouldn't drink liquor. However, ten years ago, when Mahesh picked up his six-months-old baby and tried to kiss her, she turned her face away, repelled by the smell of alcohol on his face. Seeing the repulsion in the baby's face, his aversion towards drinking became ignited. That was it. He never drank again. In all these years, he hasn't drunk a drop of alcohol. That's how aversion should arise.

UG claims that you won't be successful in practicing it [*relinquishing*] a little at a time. It must happen all at once. It's the same with anything in life. "*Sanaih, sanaih*" [*slowly, slowly*], which the Bhagavad Gita preaches is a pure lie, he says. Things must happen in one stroke. It is not a matter of time. If it happens, it must happen totally; it [*the habit*] must leave without a trace; or else, it doesn't happen at all. It's foolish to think that it can be achieved through stages.

"Did you ever have such an experience in your life? Did an event occur when you collapsed?" asked Mohan. "You want to hear about it? Are you ready?" asking him twice, UG told us about his "one-night stand". "With the experience of that one night, the sexual urge in me was completely extinguished. After that, all these forty years I haven't had any sex," said UG. He even dropped sexual intercourse with his wife. "Not just sex, but the whole pleasure movement was wiped out with it," said UG. It became clear to him that "I have no other way of gaining pleasure except by using another person for my pleasure." UG was reluctant to depend on another person for his enjoyment. He was turned off by such a situation even if the other person willingly participated. That's why his whole life, at every stage, was a field of torture.

Toward the end of the dialogue, Mohan said, "This body is nothing but a robot, nothing else; that's clear to me."

"How could it be so? You who are going to do that thing lying by your wife's side, how could that statement be real to you?" UG challenged him. Mohan shut up.

* * *

I must tear into the ego within myself and look at it. This pen of mine is my weapon. Nothing is more powerful than this. This book is the battlefield. I must wage this duel with myself without any help. In this private war, this ego is an entity to reckon with. He appears before me in my own shape. At times he prostrates before me and pleads for mercy. The next moment, he mocks demonically, pounces on me and throws me down. He makes everything topsy-turvy. He makes people who are close to me turn against me. Then I have no choice except to seek the UG Force. With the shield of remembering UG, I can guard myself. Must this struggle go on like this?

* * *

Tim's Telephone Call

Even though I have started writing, the bother of mosquitoes has not diminished. Suguna is making coffee. I won't feel settled until it goes into my stomach. This morning Tim called from London. He is eager to talk to UG. He had called in the Farm House earlier and talked to UG. "Don't come to Switzerland. Money is important. Save it," UG told him. Today, Tim asked me on the phone, "Do you know Yehudi Menuhin?" I said I did. "Does UG know that he has died a couple of days ago?" he asked. I answered, "He probably doesn't." He urged that I inform UG about it. I agreed and he hung up.

This Tim is a strange character. How UG attracts such people! They have complete liberty with UG. He goes into their world. He has the knack of going into anyone's world he wants to. The next moment he goes into someone else's world. That's why each person around him thinks that UG is moving in his or her own world, just as Krishna did in the Rasa sport in Brindavan.

Bharati's New Year's Greetings

March 18, 1999, Thursday - Telugu New Year's Day

"Tomorrow is New Year's. It's the beginning of a new era," I said to Mahesh. He looked surprised and asked, "Is that true, UG?" as if wondering if that's the true meaning of the word. "Tomorrow will be exactly like today, I guarantee you," answered UG. That may be true. But yesterday was new moon day and today is the first day of the lunar month.

As I was writing this, I got a call from Bharati. "New Year's Greetings," she said. If she picks up the phone, she doesn't put it down for at least half-an-hour. It's the same today. As UG's phone was busy, she called me. She told me that JK had explained to her UG's real nature. "He [JK] taught me about UG's state -- his ferociousness, his putting down everything, his gathering fools around him, his destroying others, his talking crazy nonsense and such other traits." She predicted that someone like Balasubrahmanya Swami [the God] would come, kick him a bit and straighten him out. "The Chinese can do such a thing, if he acts crazy. Ask him to beware," she warned. She gave him the title of "Innocent Idiot". "That too is a trait of Kala Bhairava [Siva]. Instead of making people's lives happy, he reduces them into mounds on the cremation ground. Indeed, he shaped his own life like that, standing in the cremation ground. The nature of Venkateswara, who is Vishnu's essence, is not like that. He has great grandeur -- pride, compassion and scholarship; regarding everyone with respect. That's why one must worship the Vishnu Principle instead of the Siva Principle," she said.

She named me a broker. I told her, "Twenty-five years ago you named me UG's "son of the mind", now you are giving me the new name of "broker"." She replied, "You can only cut glass with glass, a diamond with another diamond. The same way, Balasubramniam will come to set him straight. There is *kalasarpa dosha* [*the defect of the Cobra of Time*] in UG's horoscope. That's why he acts so crazy. That's the same problem with all those who were born in the sign of Gemini. My father doesn't have that grandeur of Venkateswara. That's why Venkateswara and Annamacharya wouldn't let him in their houses," she said. She continued, "Sharmila is a great person. I found the "Jabala Principle" manifested in her." "She is a great princess, truly. My husband Rayudu sits quietly in front of her and listens to what she has to say. Today is New Year's Day. That's why I felt like calling." Then she said in conclusion. "No one here is eager to see my father. Tell him it's all right if he doesn't want to come."

* * *

Mahesh: "Let my mother go..."

March 20, 1999, Saturday

Morning 4:15 a.m. After I lit the *Good Night* mosquito repellent, surprisingly, all the mosquitoes have disappeared. What happened to them? All is quiet except for the noise of the fan in Shyamalamma's room. The fan noise is rhythmic like a sound of a tomcat snoring. I hear the noise of dogs barking at a distance. This tranquil atmosphere will all change in a few minutes. A commotion will start. As the sky turns crimson, there will be increased movement of people on the street.

Today Saraswati worship is scheduled for the School children. They have examinations from the 26th. The School closes on April 10*th*. I don't have the free time to look after the School affairs. My whole day is spent with UG. From the moment I get up, there are phone calls. Then preparations are under way to go to the Farm House. The whole day is occupied with spending time with the friends who have come to see UG and making arrangements for those who are yet to come. Bob is leaving this afternoon for Madras. Shekhawat is also going to Bombay on the morning Sahara flight.

Yesterday, early in the morning, Mahesh phoned from Indore.

The man who went to Bombay at 9 p.m., two nights ago surfaced the next morning in Indore. He is attending some conference there.

This time I find again in Mahesh the earlier enthusiasm and interest. Even last December in Palm Springs, he looked dull and depressed, living in his own world, always holding a book in his hand. Although he seemed a bit more cheerful when UG was around, something appeared to be lacking.

I have noticed significant changes in Mahesh's demeanour in the last couple of years. This time, however, the old Mahesh is back in force. Huge shouts, quarrels with UG, boisterous laughing, joking around with UG and teasing -- the liberties he takes with UG no one else can. Only Mahesh is capable of goading, egging UG on, even when UG makes fun of him in front of everyone saying, "You are a real bastard." There must be a mention of money at least once each hour. When UG says, "I put your name as the beneficiary for the 10 million rupees deposit in the Canara Bank. You can have it when I die," Mahesh asks very seriously, putting his face inches from UG's face, "UG, when are you going to die?"

"I took two years' interest of 25 lakhs of rupees and made an additional deposit. These 25 lakhs will be added to the principal of 10 million rupees in two years. Until then you won't get any interest," said UG.

* * *

UG kept Mahesh's mother alive for two years. It was probably in April 1996, exactly on the Telugu New Year's Day, that UG called Mahesh to come to Bangalore to see the Farm House and our new house. Meanwhile, Mahesh's mother's illness had turned serious. Mahesh got the news from Bombay that she was in the ICU on her deathbed; so he hurried to go back. "You don't worry about your mother. I will keep her alive as long as you want. But you must pay me US$5,000 a day," said UG "I can't pay so much. I can manage Rs.5, 000 a day," answered Mahesh. UG agreed. His mother returned home safely from the ICU. Last year, when UG was staying in the flat above her flat in Bombay, she saw UG and talked to him. In these two years, the amount of the money Mahesh owed to UG grew like sin. One day, he pleaded with UG, "That's enough, UG, of keeping my mother alive. I can't pay you at the rate of Rs.5, 000 a day. Let her go."

In 1998, a month after UG left Bombay, probably in April, Mahesh's mother had died. Apparently she complained to Mahesh before she died, "You have been friends with such a great man for so many years; but you haven't acquired even a thousandth of his good traits. Is this how you treat such a guest?"

She asked UG, "I am thinking of donating my dead body to a hospital. What do you say?" "Don't. You should never help medical technology. Whatever they learn from your body they will utilise for the destruction of mankind," UG said and stopped her.

Since she died, there has been a great change in Mahesh. He produced the movie, Zakhm, based on her life. I haven't seen it yet. He said he would send me a videotape of it.

* * *

"You are fighting with yourself..."

March 20, 1999

I heard that yesterday a Californian called Robert came to the Farm House. He has been phoning me for a week trying to find a way of meeting UG. He also met Bob Carr in his hotel. Not heeding Bob's advice that it would not be good for him to meet UG, he met UG yesterday morning at 9:00 a.m. along with his wife. Major certified that he is a true *sadhaka* and that he not only has respect for human values but has dedicated his life to them wholeheartedly. He is a physicist. What else could UG wish for? It was like shaking a red cloth in front of a horned bull. After an hour-and-a-half of listening to UG's tirade against human culture, traditions, sentiments and so on, the stranger pounced on UG in anger: "Your approach is all negative. All this time I have been listening to you, not a single positive thought has come out of you. It's shameful for a realised man like you to talk disgustingly like that!"

In response, UG started condemning science and scientists. Robert was further inflamed by this and started stamping around in anger. "I didn't invite you here; you came on your own. If you don't like to hear what I have to say, you can leave," UG told him. When UG talked to him in that fashion, he apparently left in fury, leaving his wife behind. She too is a spiritual aspirant. She knows about her husband well, as Suguna knows about me. She apologised to UG for her husband's behaviour. "This is nothing new to me. You don't know how many people like this I see every day. I am not hurt by his reaction," UG consoled her. "My husband is a very good man; he has a good heart. This is the first time I have seen him like this," she said. UG knew. "That conduct is his true nature. What everyone usually sees is the façade he deliberately puts on. He won't go anywhere. He'll come back," said UG smiling.

That's the problem. You can fight someone who is openly attacking you. UG, however, subtly provokes you, incites your anger and makes you arm yourself, and when you are in the arena, he would switch to your side, thus creating the illusion that you are fighting with yourself – that's UG's way. That makes people even more crazier.

* * *

The Story of Shekhawat

The bother of the mosquitoes has subsided, thanks to this repellent. I can now write in comfort. I have written exactly for an hour. Who will benefit from what I have written so far? Who cares? I just feel happy writing. What do I care who will benefit from it? I like to keep writing like this. The pages in the book will be filled.

I feel like writing the story of B. S. Shekhawat. He has spent the past three days happily here. A couple of days ago, he was sitting with Mahesh, before UG, asking all sorts of questions. When UG asked, "Where is your wife?" his counter question was, "Which one are you referring to?" We all broke out into laughter. "I have divorced two of them already," he said.

Last night, while standing out, he told Suguna, Venkata Chalapati and me, about his married lives. I was amazed at the felicity with which he could narrate smoothly, like in a movie, the events of his life. A major facet of Shekhawat's life was revealed before our eyes. I could understand why he is so keen about UG.

Twenty years ago, Shekhawat worked as an officer in the Reserve Bank of India, Bangalore. He, with his pretty wife, used to come from Rajajinagar to 23 West Anjaneya Street, to see UG. In the days when Mahesh and Parveen lived here, he too came frequently.

It was in those times that he married Kumud Rathore, the daughter of a royal family of a province called Kota in Rajasthan. He was from a middle class family while she was a princess. The marriage occurred at the behest of the Queen Mother of Mysore, in a way; because he had declined a proposal from the Mysore royal family. He didn't want royalty to rule his personal life, too. The Rathore family knew about it and never disclosed their roots to him before the wedding day! He didn't know of the princess's status before the marriage. They showed him the girl in a farmhouse in Delhi. The wedding took place in Kota. The palace there had 40 rooms in it. There were many servants. The grounds of the palace were huge. There were fabulous gates. He marvelled at all this, riding on a horse on the wedding day and wondering whether he was awake or dreaming. He was worried that they might have duped him into marrying an old lady; so immediately after the wedding, he lifted the veil of the bride. He saw her beautiful face and heaved a sigh of relief. But his joy was short-lived.

How could Kumud, who grew up in princely luxuries, take to a common middle class lifestyle? Our hero found a house for them to live in Bangalore. He handed over his first month's salary, then a princely sum of Rs. 2,700 to her. In three days, she demanded more money to run the house. All the money he gave her had disappeared. Shekhawat almost fainted. His wife blew up a whole month's salary in three days. In addition, she spent some of her own money. There were four servants in the house. She could cook well, but she needed servants to help her in the cooking. She also needed servants to clean, wash clothes, arrange things in the house and run errands outside home. Their married life survived for three years. She got tired of it.

And then one day, UG told her, in Shekhawat's presence, "What are you doing here with this man, royal lady? Quit!" So she grabbed their son and moved back to Kota. Now the boy is 17-years-old. They divorced, with a smile! The two still relate to each other as friends. Each year, at least once or twice, they meet and spend time together.

Meanwhile, Shekhawat's acquaintance with a young colleague,

a girl 10 years younger than him, an officer in his bank, NABARD, turned into romance. Shekhawat used to endlessly talk to her about UG. When they came to see UG in Delhi, UG asked the lady, "Why do you want to marry this guy? You are young, pretty and in a good job!" So they happily "lived in sin" for two and half years in Jaipur. Unfortunately, they decided to marry. But they soon realised that they couldn't live together out of sin. The thrill was gone! They applied for divorce at the end of first year. The judge couldn't understand why these two, who were so friendly to each other, wanted to divorce. Was it for the sake of property? They said that wasn't the reason. They lived together happily before marriage and divorced happily a year after their marriage. "So there are two "Mrs. Shekhawats" now," he says. The Delhi lady too sees him sometimes. She asks him about his life. She still works in the same bank.

Meanwhile, he was transferred to Jammu & Kashmir. In Srinagar some extremists thought that Shekhawat was a Muslim because "Shakhawat" is also a Muslim name. When Bhairon Singh Shekhawat became the Chief Minister of Rajasthan, it became known to everyone there that our Shekhawat was also from the same family. His family links to the BJP stalwart became public. It was no longer safe to be in J&K. He was soon after transferred to Bombay.

And then there was a failed love story in Bombay.

He casually met this receptionist working in a five star hotel, this time 15 years younger than him. They hit off instantly. He told her all the details of his life without hiding anything. She said she wanted to talk to his first wife and took her phone number from him. "Just like a person talks to a previous owner before he buys a second-hand car to find out if it had any problems, she wanted to gather details about me from my first wife," says Shekhawat. The two talked to each other over STD for an hour-and-a-half. No matter how long, or how cleverly, she discussed with his first wife, this young lady could not find out what his faults were and why they divorced. "If you want to marry him, do it quickly. Or else he may change his mind," advised the princess. "She is still immensely fond of you. How can I marry you? It won't work. This is the end of our relationship" said the young lady. In two weeks, the lady said goodbye to Shekhawat. "She is the only one whom I could not introduce to UG", says Shekhawat regretfully.

Since then, Shekhawat remained single for many years. Still, while these things had been happening, he never quit his contact with Mahesh or his relationship with UG or me. That's his saving grace. In every way, UG's support to Shekhawat remains intact.

Post-script:

Shekhawat once again got involved with a TV actress, whom he met when she was an airhostess, this time a good 20 years younger than him! The lady loved this 'prince'. Their acquaintance ended in marriage. During one of their visits to UG in Bombay, UG had joked with her, saying, "You are pretty, young, rich and talented. Why are you hanging around this much married man?" She seemed to have taken the joke seriously. This marriage too ended in divorce in 2009.

Now, with UG gone in 2007, Shekhawat has only UG, -- no wife! "Wives come and go; UG is eternal", says Shekhawat.

* * *

"I don't give any importance to my opinions...."

March 25, 1999

It was 3 p.m. It was very hot in Chennai. We were all staying in Malladi Krishnamurti's house. Most of the time during the day, one would prefer to stay indoors, in an air-conditioned room. However, despite the heat outside, UG wanted to see the new supermarket, "Maya Plaza", in Pondy Bazaar.

That night, about thirty people gathered on the terrace of Krishnamurti's house to meet with UG. One young man named Koteswar came with his friend. They were both from the Krishnamurti Foundation of India. They both seemed eager to ask UG a lot of questions. But UG seemed not to be in a mood to discuss serious questions. I thought he might take a break in the middle. But he narrated the whole JK story for more than an hour, without giving people a chance to ask any questions: "I have unbounded admiration for him [JK] now, not for his teaching or what he did in his life, but for the way he kept everything under the rug so successfully. Normally, when there is more than one woman involved, jealousies or things like that are bound to occur. The affairs are bound come to light. But he, like a US navy man, had a girl in every port and kept everything secret very successfully. I have unbounded admiration for that!" he said. He thus recited his JK obituary and concluded his story. Some ladies next to me whispered to each other, "It seems that UG doesn't like JK at all."

The friends from the Krishnamurti Foundation of India, however, seemed to have enjoyed it. One of them asked UG, "You seem to have a lot of opinions."

"I have opinions on everything, from disease to divinity."

"Then what's the difference between me and you? I too have opinions."

"Absolutely no difference. Only you seem to give a lot of importance to your opinions and I don't. That's all," UG said.

* * *

The trouble the Delhi lady went through to meet UG...

March 28, 1999

Sunny, a young lady from Delhi came to Bangalore with a friend called Roma to see UG. She first talked to Archana on the phone and learned that we were returning from Madras Friday night. So they both arrived in Bangalore Thursday night by air. Meanwhile, our phone was broken. So, no matter how often she tried, the phone never rang. The two worked hard for three hours and finally found our house with the help of the address they had. I called and talked to her from Chalapati's house. I asked her to come to the Farm House in the afternoon at around 3 p.m.

There she told me how she had searched the whole world trying to meet UG. She bought UG's book *Mystique* on February 14, 1998 at a book exhibition in Delhi. She was fascinated by UG's disclaimer on the first page. So she has been hunting for UG ever since. That day it happened to be Valentine's Day. She learned later that Valentine was UG's support; so she thought she was very fortunate to have found that book on Valentine's day.

Last April, she went on a vacation to Europe and America with her friend. At that time, she didn't know anything more about UG except what she had read in the book. Meanwhile, she saw the books I had sent to the Reiki master, Nilam Sood. When she went to

Switzerland she remembered that UG stays in Saanen. From Geneva she went to Montreau and from there to Gstaad. But at that time she didn't know that UG was in Gstaad. *Mystique* only mentions Saanen. She went around all over Saanen, with that book in her hand, looking for UG. People there said they didn't know him. She knew that JK also used to come there. So she wrote 'UG' in big letters on a paper and asked people about him. But she had no luck.

When she came to the US from there, she went around New York, San Francisco, Los Angeles and Carmel -- all those places where UG had stayed sometime or other. Still she couldn't find a trace of him. After she came to Delhi, while she was attending a meeting of a man called Diljit, she heard Frank Noronha talking about Mahesh Bhatt and UG. Sunny got hold of Frank and obtained my number from him. She called and talked to me and finally her desire was fulfilled after so much time and effort.

* * *

March 29, 1999, Monday

Today is the Muslim festival of Bakrid. It's a national holiday. Morning 5:30 a.m. I was writing yesterday about Sunny. She phoned again yesterday. She must have left for Delhi on the evening flight yesterday. "I came with the idea of meeting UG and having a chat with him. I was very satisfied having met him and talked to him, all of it. I am very thankful to you for creating such an opportunity and cooperating. You must certainly look me up if you ever come to Delhi," she told me on the phone and said goodbye.

I don't know why, but whenever I see her or hear her words, I am reminded of Kameswari. Many years ago, a lady appeared in my dream, who looked exactly like Sunny, and I remember UG referring to her as "the Western version of Kameswari".

Sunny's dress and appearance were also Western. She wore a skirt and a blouse, and had long loose hair, just like Parveen. She was attractive. She didn't express any interest in seeing UG again. I gave her and her friend a copy each of *Courage* and Larry's book of poetry.

* * *

The *Idiappam* Story

I must write about the story of *idiappam* that took place yesterday. Earlier, in the days when UG was living in Yercaud, the postmaster there used to make *idiappam* and bring it over. His wife prepared it well. I still don't understand why the Tamils are so fond of that dish. Major simply abhors it. It's stringy and coiled like *semia*. They say it's pretty tedious to make it. It's supposed to be eaten with coconut milk. Even if you mix it with that milk, we don't know what kind of taste it will have.

It's not clear whether UG liked to eat it, but he mentioned it once during a conversation with a friend called Suguna Krishnamurti. She lives in Jayanagar. She doesn't seem to be older than 30, but she is not married yet. She is a chartered accountant. She lost her father and lives with her mother. She has been coming to see UG for the last three years. Even at times when UG is not here, she would come to our home occasionally, borrow UG's audio tapes and return them. She is stunningly beautiful. You can't take your eyes off her. How innocent she looks! Yet, she is just as intelligent as she is good-looking. She even lectures in some colleges as part of her profession. She probably told us the background of her being attracted to UG, but I can't remember.

She knows how to make *idiappam*. Perhaps she thought that it was something UG is very fond of. The last time she had come she made it and brought it over. She first told us she was going to make it, but brought it over to the Farm House after quite a while. Major hates that dish. "You call that edible! How could they eat such a thing?" he says. That time, even UG finally gave away the remnants of the dish to Ammmayamma after keeping it for two days.

Last night, Suguna Krishnamurti phoned. Major answered. She asked if she could make some *idiappam* for UG and bring it over. Major's face shrank when he heard the name of that dish. He was furious. "There is no need for any such thing. You come, that's good enough," he said, sounding annoyed. Although UG was trying to tell him in the background that if she had made *idiappam* she should bring it with her, Major wouldn't listen; instead, he told her that UG doesn't like that dish and asked her not to bring it.

UG asked him, "How do you know that I don't like it?"

"Did you eat what she brought the last time? You gave it away to Ammayamma. I remember very well. Why should she go to great pains to make that dish and push it on us?" Major told everyone whatever had happened the last time.

But UG didn't agree: "I am eating your *upma*, what more proof do you want that I can eat any kind of dish?" he challenged. "You phone her and tell her; if she has *idiappam* ready, ask her to bring it," he insisted. He didn't give up until Major phoned Suguna Krishnamurti and asked her to come.

My wife Suguna also phoned her, talked to her and asked her to bring *idiappam*. The lady prepared it right after that and brought it around 5 p.m. on her scooter.

When everyone was leaving at 6 p.m., UG asked Suguna Krishnamurti to wait and said, "This Major told you some nonsense. I'll eat your *idiappam* right in your presence. You can leave after I eat." That made everyone laugh. Suguna Krishnamurti was afraid that her *idiappam* had brought trouble to UG.

"If you don't like to eat what I have made, I won't bring it again, UG," she said apologetically, appearing to be hurt.

"No, no, nothing of the sort. I like it. Watch me. I will eat right in your presence," he said and served himself.

I thought that from now on Suguna Krishnamurti's *idiappam* is going to become a tradition for UG.

Venkata Chalapati was astounded by all this: "Look how delicate UG's nature is. He thought she might feel hurt; so he made sure she brought it and ate it right in front of her. In words, however, he says, 'I am a cruel butcher; I don't have any affection; I have fondness for no one; mine is a stony heart; I have no mercy.' But actually, see how compassionate he is!" he marvelled.

But we can't assume that UG acts so compassionately in all contexts. Everyone knows that too. Everything depends on the situation. We cannot generalise and say that he will act the same way in all situations.

* * *

The Way of UG's Health

We are awestruck with UG. His body is never subject to disease. Even though he travels to different countries and continents, colds, coughs, headaches and so on never afflict him. In earlier times, however, every time he came to India, he used to be laid down with the flu. He never took medicines. He would just eat less than normal. Even in the height of fever, he never stopped his normal activities. He hasn't had such a fever for the last fifteen years. Even the alimentary canal has not been bothering him so much. Before, he used to have a problem with a hernia. It doesn't look like he has that problem now. He can travel with ease for hours on end in a car. He doesn't rest. He doesn't even take a little nap after lunch. At times, however, he dozes off while sitting on the sofa even when someone is talking.

One day, Mr. Narasimha Reddi was talking about the ashram of Sai Baba. While he was talking about sundry other things, UG dozed off on the sofa. That much rest is adequate for him. On the other hand, I need three days to recover after he leaves. During the days he is here, I feel as if I am deprived of full sleep. He has many urgent affairs to attend to. Many people surround him. He has to listen to their problems and complaints. UG doesn't get tired of them. Doesn't his body get tired? How can he always remain fresh like a flower? Wouldn't he get tired after talking for hours and hours? For hours at a time, he doesn't get out of that chair. People still keep coming. Those who have to leave, say goodbye and leave unwillingly. UG never gets tired. He has no rest and he is never tired. How can his body withstand all that, his 82-year-old body? Where does he get all that energy from? Where do his words get all that force? He eats so little.

UG's body itself is a wonder. His hair has been turning dark in the last couple of years. There are now some very dark strands of hair, which had been completely grey before. How is that possible? It's a wonder to everyone.

The lines in his palms have been changing. The "heart line" in his right hand broke up and changed into an "M" shape. People have been interpreting that "M" in different ways: as the Mars that is approaching, money, mission, master and so on. Whatever it might mean, the letter appears clearly in his palm. All the lines in his palm point to the index finger.

* * *

UG - an inspiration for an American Reiki Guru

May 9, 1999 – Sunday

In a daily newspaper called *Business Line*, there is an article on the topic of "Reiki – the Mystical Energy", talking about an American Reiki guru called Paula Horan. A lady named Priti Mohra wrote it. In it, Paula Horan mentions the discussion she had with UG many years ago and recalls UG's words. She says that if you want to increase the effect of "Reiki", you must get out of the "I, me and myself" syndrome; you should stop being concerned about yourself, you should understand the life of "being in the world but not of it." She says that she has assimilated such important principles of living from her conversation with UG.

* * *

Political Climate

May 18-19, Tuesday and Wednesday

I am resuming the diary exactly after nine days. I didn't think that the writing would take a back seat while UG is here. I had a high fever on 12th and 13th. Pulandar diagnosed it as a viral fever and gave me homeopathic medicines which have brought it down. Then I was pretty weak till last Sunday. Meanwhile, Suguna and Archana too got the fever. By the time they have recovered it was already Monday. This time the three of them competed with each other and got fevers which hit 103–103.5°. Pulandar helped us out by coming twice a day, giving us medicines and reassurance.

Meanwhile, last Friday, on the 14th, YNK came with five of his associates and interviewed UG. Apparently, Mr. Ranganath, a senior editor, talked to UG. That evening, there was torrential rain at the Farm House. As a matter of fact, for the last ten days, it has become a routine each day for the skies to become overcast in the evenings and rain heavily in the nights. With UG's arrival, the weather has changed to the extent that you wondered if this is really summer!

The political climate in the country too has been changing from day to day. The Congress Party electing Sonia Gandhi as its leader broke the backbone of all the old jackals [*old guard*]. The Party's members have made it their life-aim to extol Sonia. Ever since UG has come to India, not an hour passed without his going on a tirade against the Congress Party. He has been severely abusing its leaders:

"Can this country, which has almost a billion people, not produce a single leader to run the nation? Must they bring that ... Sonia from Italy to be the prime minister? Have you become so used to the life of slavery that your blood has cooled down? Aren't you ashamed of yourselves? How could you tolerate it? The Congress Party is the root cause of all this. There is no hope for your nation unless the Congress Party is destroyed to the roots," UG has thus been jabbing at them and pouncing on them.

He knows that my father supports the Congress Party; so he shouts especially when he is present. He condemns Gandhi and vilifies him. He pours abuse on Nehru and the Nehru dynasty and says that Nehru was the sole cause of the downfall of this country. He uses all the foul language at his command, without repeating himself, to condemn the Nehru dynasty.

Apparently, Nagesh's family came to listen to him; but seeing his ferocious visage, they got terrified and left. "Why would a realised man become so emotional? If he doesn't like something, he could indicate it gently. Why use this foul language?"that's how Nagesh reasoned and then left. UG doesn't care about what people think. "Sonia must not grab the power!" he was screaming his head off. His manner is the same whether he talks in the Farm House or here -- terribly foul language.

Suddenly there is a movement in the country. Chandrababu Naidu waved his flag by personally attacking Sonia Gandhi. Some others joined their voices to his. Meanwhile, there is some other crisis afoot in the Congress Party. Three leaders, Sarad Pawar, Sangama and Tariq Anvir, blew their horns of rebellion. They wrote a long letter to Sonia claiming that foreigners have no right to occupy the highest seat in this country and demanding that she should immediately desist from her efforts to become the prime minister. With that letter politics here has taken a new turn.

Monday, UG bought his ticket for travel. He will leave next Friday evening at 6 p.m. That means that he will be in Bangalore for another 10 days. There are going to be innumerable changes during these 10 days.

Whenever you see or hear anything—on TV, on radio, or in the newspapers—there is only the talk of rebellion against Sonia Gandhi. Sonia Gandhi resigned from her chairmanship. She gathered all her money. Everyone has been making noise. They have cast out the three people who created this crisis and have condemned them in every possible way. These are the storm-winds that UG has anticipated. The Congress Party must be levelled. Sonia Gandhi must exit the stage taking her progeny with her.

* * *

UG in YNK's Office

UG stepped into the *Indian Express* office on Monday at noon. YNK welcomed him into his office and said, feeling flattered, "Fifteen years ago, when I was in *Praja Vani*, Ambarish Verma [Mr. *YNK's one-time mystic guru who is now deceased*] came. Today, UG has set his foot in my office." UG remarked, "Your office seems to be a happy mixture of the old and the new." YNK told him, "We can't give you the tape of the interview yet. It must first be published in the paper." Then he joked, "'Dynasty' is an indication to 'die nasty'." UG jumped with joy for finding the use of such a sharp phrase. Since then he has been using the phrase "die nasty". He warns, "If Sonia behaves foolishly and doesn't get off the stage, she must be prepared to die mercilessly along with her children."

* * *

May 27, Thursday

"Get along or get lost…"

UG stayed home all day. … He has been talking most all the

time as usual. He paused once and pounced on me, while I was arranging books in the bookshelf, pointing out that I wasn't doing anything about the videotapes. What can I do? I don't have an ounce of enthusiasm. I am not interested in anything. I don't even know what's happening to me.

Yesterday, while we were going to Satyanarayana's house in the car, I asked UG if he had ever suffered from sadness, depression or anxiety before his "Calamity". "Your problem is not life. Living together is your problem. You worry about how to maintain relationships. I never worried about that. My attention was always on how to face the situation in front of me. I never even bothered to find out how I got involved in such a situation or what caused it. "This is the situation now and how do I proceed from here? What should I do?" That's all I thought about—to overcome it. And I never lost."

Even when he was little, even when he was under his grandfather's care, he only knew how to get his way and how to move away, if he couldn't. He was not bothered by the problems which normally afflict men. He never had problems. He always tried to turn people around him in the direction favourable to him. Those who did not agree with him had no place near him. It's the same even now. "Get along or get lost," is his motto.

* * *

Political Outrage

May 28, 1999, Friday

Just as I was about to start writing, I looked at the date printed on this page of the diary. It was UG's birthday! I want to get my book *Stopped in Our Tracks* printed and released by his birthday this year. I should mention that to UG. Just a little over a month remains. Meanwhile, who knows through how many countries he will roam? He says he won't come back to India unless Sonia exits. He says that this time he will go to Italy just on the mission of finding out and revealing Sonia's secrets. He says he will start his tirade against India on the TV there. Yesterday morning, as soon as he came home, while he was upstairs, he started screaming in a big way. Not just against Sonia Gandhi, but also abusing this nation as a whole, saying that it's a useless country. "India has a billion people. Still, I can't find a single person here who has self-respect. NATO bombs fell on the Indian embassy in Belgrade; a low-level official in the NATO Forces noted that it was "our mistake" and didn't even apologise. Then, fifteen days ago, a bomb fell on the Chinese embassy, destroying it. The Chinese leaders couldn't contain their anger. The American President Clinton personally apologised to the Chinese people three times in public meetings. High-level officials from the American Department of State went to China to explain in detail to the Chinese leaders how the mistake had occurred. They begged the Chinese for their forgiveness. But they don't care about the Indians, because our status is so low. Let alone having any high regard for people or leaders of this country, they just don't give a damn."

UG has been saying that unless they have economic power and military might, no country will gain recognition. "It's useless to blame this country. It doesn't have the right leadership. It needs someone like Mao Tse Tung. But there is no one here like that. Gandhi and Nehru let the country down. Later, the Congress Party used both of them to maintain its power; furthermore, it put the Nehru dynasty in power and thereby, did enormous treachery."

He has been going on like this. Yesterday, in the afternoon and in the evening, there was a large crowd in the living room.

Nagesh's entire family was present. Their daughter kept quiet before UG. She appeared to be angry for some reason. It's hard to tell whom and how UG's words affect. We watched the video *What am I saying?* It was great. I felt like seeing it again and again. We also watched an Australian videotape, an edited version. In it, UG spoke very little.

* * *

Political Outrage – ii

May 29, 1999

Last evening, around 6 p.m., UG left for Bombay on Jet Airways. From there, he must have left for Frankfurt on Lufthansa at 2:30 a.m. By this time, he would be in Germany, criticising India and Sonia Gandhi. He called at 10 p.m. last night from Mahesh's home in Bombay.

He mentioned some new facts about Kashmir revealed by Shekhawat. He explained that the military conflict in Kargil is only a "storm in the teacup" created by the BJP Party. Apparently, Kargil was the place of Nehru's and Kamala's honeymoon. That's why

Nehru had insisted on having Kashmir as part of India.

Now, the Pakistanis have been shooting rockets from the occupied part of Kashmir. Recently, they shot down two MIG planes. Yesterday, they destroyed a helicopter. The war is taking a serious turn. There are rumours that all these incidents are deliberately instigated by the Vajpayee Government.

Whatever it is, UG has been busy initiating a movement from foreign soil. He has vowed that he will see the end of Sonia. Where does he get such passion and energy? It's amazing.

Day by day, I have been getting weaker. I have been feeling increasingly lazy. Meanwhile UG's energy has been shooting up. Each day, the whole house resonates with his shouts: "You are all cowards, spineless people and a bunch of slaves!" he has been scolding the Indians. "How can you tolerate such a party like Congress? It should be wiped off from the face of this earth... ," he said.

It would be no wonder that anyone listening to this might think that UG hates everyone. When Suguna Krishnamurti asked him, "Why are you so mad at them? Why do you launch such a tirade against Sonia Gandhi?" he pounced on her. This whole month he has only been talking politics. This is the first time in years that UG has been expressing his anger at Sonia in the newspapers. "The first misfortune of India is Gandhi and the second is Nehru. It is its misfortune that no leader like Mao has been born in this country," says UG. "If India and China would join hands, they could put a stop to an evil country like America. But now China is the only strong country that can stand up to America. There is a lot that India has to learn from China," he says. But you can't trust China. The Chinese have gained a reputation as the foremost in being treacherous. They deceived us in 1962. Even now, no matter how well their country has done, their tongues are forked. Still, UG has been praising China. He not only praises it, but he talks as if there is no other country on earth greater than China. He depicts America as an evil force and a pest on this earth.

* * *

UG's Ways

May 30, 1999, Sunday

He who is ready to die at any moment will live forever. There will be no death for him. He will have no life of his own. He will have no existence called "himself". Each moment he watches the magic of the Lord of Arunchala, without a consciousness that he is separate from it. He lives fully and is fulfilled every moment.

"I am always fully occupied with whatever is happening at any given point of time. So, I am never pre-occupied with other things," says UG. In so many ways he makes this clear to us! Someone's leg moving, hands swinging, pigeons taking off from a tree, lizards making sounds on the wall – these are enough to fill the whole of his being. Without there being a "he", he is completely merged from moment to moment with whatever is happening in his presence. He talks, he scolds, he gets angry, he makes fun, he laughs and makes others laugh; he pours forth his compassion or he behaves harshly; he jumps from one subject matter to another without any connection; he speaks, shattering others' arguments with his logic; yet throughout he remains as if nothing concerns him. He interferes in some people's personal affairs even if they don't like it. With some others, even if they plead, he wouldn't bother even to look at them. I can go on and on writing like this about UG's ways. We can call such a man an enlightened man, "one who is released while still alive", a realised man or a jñani. We can use many terms like this. But you can never understand such people. They don't fit within our limited frames. "Oh, is that all? I understand all about them" — by the time we come to think this way, they will laugh at us and they tease us by breaking out of our imagined frame.

UG will never let you know who is nearer to him and who is distant from him. Sometimes, he appears as if his judgments are blind and totally prejudiced. Sometimes, he makes you feel that his words are literally true. Some other times, he makes you feel that "there is nothing more exaggerated than this." Some will condemn his words right in front of him. They reconcile themselves thinking that that's his disposition. Some he blames constantly without any apparent reason and makes fun of them in front of everyone; he brushes them off as useless. And there are others he praises whether they have done or not done anything special; he extols them in front of everyone. Some whom he extols today, he puts down the next day. He makes you feel, "The realised man's mind moves from moment to moment." You feel that the mind of the mindless man acts as it pleases. But he is not affected by anything he does. Even if others praise it or suffer from it, cry about it or laugh about it, even if they act in anger or spite, even if they blame him and abuse him and even if they submit themselves to him saying he is their only help – none of that touches him. Nothing stays with him.

* * *

"If you understand what I am saying at all, you wouldn't look at my face..."

May 31, 1999, Monday

"Although a great treasure fell into my hands, my sinful mind goes after pots and herds," wails Chalam's Yashoda in his *Yashoda Gitalu*. Not just her mind, but the minds of many such "fortunate" people have been landing on garbage heaps for generations, from times immemorial; they have indeed set up permanent residences there.

Last night, Gopala Naidu called from Hyderabad and mentioned how UG through his compassionate conversation had dispersed multitudes of doubts he had accumulated in his mind. He told me that if there is anything most urgent that needs to be done in his life, it is to spend time in UG's presence.

I used to feel like that often before. But now? Even though such a good fortune as UG stands right at my doorstep, I do indeed run far away from it on some pretext or other. Why have I changed like that? Why is it that the truths, realities and words of experience beyond the mind, which he teaches, don't operate in my mind?

In the article by Mahesh Bhatt that came out yesterday, "Zen and the Art of Imitation" he recounts a Zen story. A teacher calls all his pupils and says "Find out what Truth is by investigating it yourselves and come back to me." He fixes a period of time for them to spend on the search and sends them off. They all return after the specified time. Each one narrates the meaning that has dawned on him and what he has understood. The teacher kindly asks one disciple who has been sitting silently with downcast eyes, "Why are you not saying anything?" "No matter how deeply and intensely I inquired, I couldn't find any answer which I could call mine. Whatever I know are the truths that others have known; I am unable to find the real truth," the disciple replies sadly. The teacher hugs him immediately in immense joy.

UG had arrived at this truth while he was still young. What is my true desire? What do I really want? "I only have assumed that the desires of those around me are mine and have been spending all my life striving to satisfy them. But what, indeed, in me is a desire which I could truly call mine?" Thus, while he was still very young, he rejected all those desires which others had known.

Although I am writing about all these things, my mind doesn't grasp their value. I must find "mine', "my way". I must first find out what my question is, what I want. I must learn by myself that that [*satisfaction*] is not possible. There is no use in repeating the truths that UG has discovered.

That's why UG so clearly says, "If you understand what I am saying at all, you wouldn't look at my face. You won't sit before me and listen to what I say. Only then you will express in your own way what you understand. And you won't follow me. You won't worship anyone. That will be the end of your story," he says.

"How true, those words!" I thought. That means I have been goofing.

* * *

Looking for Causes...

June 4, 1999, Friday

It has become a habit of mine to look for a cause for every event and connect it to the event; to constantly ask myself, "What's the cause of whatever has happened? Perhaps it happened that way because I thought that way;" to feel happy thinking that things have turned out well because of the precautions I had taken; or to be disappointed with myself that something untoward has happened because of some negligence of mine – this kind of thinking has become part of my daily routine.

Yesterday, Viswanath, the driver, questioned me about UG's philosophy while we were driving in the car to take it down to the shop for repairs. Two evenings ago, when I was driving the car, it hit a tree and the gears on the front axle were damaged. I have been asking myself the question "Why did it happen like that?" over and over again. I haven't stopped asking it yet. The question has been haunting me. It doesn't go away.

Viswanath also asked the same sort of question regarding the way UG acts. Apparently, he went upstairs to say goodbye to UG. As Viswanath was leaving, UG said, "Say hello to your wife; she came with you the other day, right?" Viswanath was extremely surprised. "With such a difference in status between UG and us, I can't even imagine that he remembers so much and asking about her," he said to me.

Viswanath's wife too was flattered when she heard about it. How could such things happen? UG doesn't think about them. Things just happen mechanically, without any involvement on his part. Nothing enters his mind except the things that happen around him at each moment. For him, every action, every event happens independently; he has lost the habit of searching for causes of events or linking events in terms of causes and effects. No one knows how that habit ceased.

If that habit is gone, it means that his whole existence is gone; because if such thoughts don't arise, there cannot be any such thing as "I" or "mine".

My reasoning is also a result of my looking for a cause-and-effect relationship. A cause-and-effect thinking is operating in my observations of UG, in my trying to understand the way he acts and explaining what I understand to others. But why should I want to get rid of this process? Is that because UG says he doesn't think in those terms? Is it because in the scriptures and Vedanta books it was mentioned that to get rid of it is to be in such a great state? Or is it because of my fear, based on my greed, that I may be missing some great experience in that state? Right now, at this moment, what am I lacking? Why should I think of UG's person as a model over and over again? Could I live even for a moment in a way natural to me? Every minute I am trying to change myself and shape myself; I exert myself to attain something that I fear I have lost – all this futile effort, who is it for? How completely have I become overpowered by such despair and helplessness! I can't stand up as me. Why? Why? Why? Why?

* * *

"Release means total destruction..."

Normally, I have great fondness and love for UG. I eagerly await his arrival. I have a strong desire to tell everyone about him and get them to see UG. Once, my worship of UG flowed into poetry in the Sisa meter. Now, I don't have any such notions; instead, ideas quite contrary to them whirl in my mind. Where do these come from? If I could at least write hostile poems about UG, that would be great. But I can't even do that.

From the moment I get up from bed, I impose various activities upon myself, always trying to test how far I can run away from this consciousness in me. I constantly try to hide from the truths that lie within me. Why am I becoming like this? And, I have fears about the future. I don't understand. Everything seems confusing.

My ego complains and says that UG is the cause of this situation. If I ask it, "What do you lack now? What are you losing right now?" it won't answer. It doesn't even know what harm has occurred or what troubles it has run into. It worries now about money problems that might possibly arise in the future.

I have decided to sell my shares [in the Finance Corporation] and gather the money needed to print my book. My ego keeps grumbling. When I say, "What do you lack now? You seem to be happy," it doesn't answer. It doesn't know what it wants. Does it want the bliss of release? Who told it that such a thing exists? Do you know what it's like? You say it's not something that can be experienced. Then how do you know about it? Isn't it the knowledge that you have gathered that's your basis of knowing? Why are you so fascinated by the image which the knowledge has created? Why are you so excited about something which you evidently do not know?

"Release means total destruction. Do you really want such destruction?" asks UG. When I heard earlier from UG directly the promise that "On whomever I bestow my grace, him I'll rob of everything," I used to plead in my mind, "I am ready. Be merciful and burn me." At that time, I didn't have much to lose. A lot of "mine" has accumulated in all these years — especially this pleasurable living, the pleasure of going to bed whenever I want, the life of culture, honour and respectability, a certain status in society and property. All these will go, if the promise of God is fulfilled.

Oh yes, I am afraid. This ego chickens out when I put it on the spot and ask, "What do you want?" That's why they said, "Only the courageous can wish for immortality." But who are those courageous ones? I can't find anyone in history except UG. Who has the strength to deliberately ruin a fruitful life? How much courage does it take? Who has the strength of heart to throw everything he has to the winds without expecting anything in return and without wanting any power and become a beggar? It's not unimaginable to let go of what one already has with the hope that one will find some higher state. It's truly a great thing to sacrifice whatever one has and not let even a thought of "how can I manage tomorrow?" enter one's mind, yet realising that one will gain nothing. UG has been the same then and now. There has been no change. My miserable nature puts on a different garb at every turn and causes troubles.

* * *

"Why do you need a philosophy to live?"

Once upon a time, I used to have a great resolve that I should formulate a philosophy of life for myself and try to live according to it to the best of my ability. My resolve broke down when UG asked, "Why do you need a philosophy to live?"

"Who are you to put life in some kind of order? Life will go its own way. Who are you to stand in its way?" UG asked me.

True, I don't have an answer. We want "Life" to mean that whatever we want and hope for must happen. "There must be only happiness and not even a trace of suffering." If life proceeds in that fashion, then we are glad and feel that life is meaningful. But there is no connection between life and the things that happen.

But mental anxieties, fears, sorrows, mental tortures, distress, cringing – all these afflict me and make me impotent. They can't touch life. Yet they possess me. They are squeezing my throat. How horrible!

If they are to destroy me, why I am sorry? Isn't that what I want?

"You don't know a thing about life. Your problem is only "how to live"." Life goes on as it pleases without being concerned about you. First, think about for whom all this anxiety exists. Find that out!

Sleep is rushing in and closing my eyelids. Time, morning 6:15 a.m. I have written for more than an hour. I am still sleepy.

* * *

"It's a game for the cat..."

I must write about an incident to illustrate how UG plays around with the people who come close to him.

Of course, we all know the story of Julie: I think it was in 1989, after she met UG for the first time, she went around the whole world with UG for almost a year. She made videos. UG was at first respectful towards her. Valentine was still alive at that time. Julie, however, couldn't maintain the status of being "needed" which UG had first accorded her. She deluded herself into thinking that UG should put her in Valentine's place. UG realised that and started pushing her away. Julie couldn't stand that and started coming in his way. With that UG started detesting Julie intensely. That disgust has been growing till today.

Guha's story is similar. He learned about UG through the Internet. He met UG and got very close to him. In these three to four years, the whole family of Guha has become dear to UG. It's not just UG everyone likes Guha's children Shilpa and Sumedha. I don't even have to mention Lakshmi, Guha's wife. Guha has no other preoccupation in life except thinking about UG. This professor who has been doing research in superconductivity in Rutgers University just forgot himself in his attraction to UG. With UG's prompting, he obtained a "Green Card" in America. But I think he gets into pretty serious depressions.

The last month while UG was here, Guha was having a difficult time in the US – he couldn't take it. He is fed up with his job. He doesn't like living in America or his life there. Yet UG doesn't let him move to India. UG insists that their children must grow up in America in that atmosphere. He has biased their minds against India deliberately. He gets furious if Guha even mentions India's name.

Guha is finding it hard to work in the university. Lakshmi says that some allergy is bothering him.

Finally, Julie phoned the Farm House one day. Major picked up the phone. She informed him, "Guha is resigning from his job and returning to Hyderabad." She asked Major to tell UG that. She thought that at least for that reason UG might be interested in talking to her. UG had already stopped talking to Guha by then. Knowing that Julie plots to come close to him by having Lakshmi and her children by her side, UG has been harsh with Lakshmi too. He has even stopped talking to the kids.

When Major reported what Julie had said, UG pounced on the Major. Then he phoned Lakshmi in anger. She told him that Guha was on leave and was saying he couldn't work at that job anymore. Then why had Julie reported like that? Was it with the idea that UG

Stopped in Our Tracks 179

would interfere? Major too got upset with Julie for telling him lies and causing UG to be angry at him.

UG spoke to Guha that day. "You have only two alternatives: you decide whether you will enter a mental hospital there, or come to Hyderabad and sit in jail here. If you don't go back to your job, one of these two consequences is certain. If you come to Hyderabad, I will use all my influence to put you in jail," he said.

Guha didn't say a word in reply. Lakshmi called once or twice to talk to UG but UG did not budge. And there was no need for him to say anything to Julie. He just didn't talk at all.

I don't know if Guha is still on leave or went back to work. UG is now in Italy. He will go to Rome to see Paulo.

Part IV

A Burglary

June 14, 1999, Monday

The dates of June 12 and 13 will remain unforgettable to me. On the night of Saturday, the 12th, around 8 p.m., a burglar or burglars entered our house. They broke the locks of the two front doors with the help of pry bars, came in and ransacked our bedroom, Archana's and father's rooms upstairs, the archives room and all. I am surprised at myself — before I had left, I felt like removing all the cash from the wooden cabinet and transferring it into the steel cabinet and locking the cabinet. Normally, even when I go on a journey for months, I would always leave the money in the wooden cabinet. I still don't understand why, this time, I felt like moving the money over to the steel cabinet and why those scoundrels didn't touch the steel cabinet but only pried open the wooden cabinets and ransacked them.

Not much is lost because of that. They took some three hundred rupees belonging to father and my Sanyo radio-tape-recorder. That was all they could find. Another surprising thing is that I had thought of taking all the cash from the wooden cabinet to Tirupati with me. I don't normally do that. Even though I knew I was returning in a day, the precautions I took this time I had never taken before even when I went away for weeks. The burglars would have profited

Stopped in Our Tracks 181

more if they had opened the steel cabinet. I must say it was their misfortune. Or should I say it was my good luck.

Why did I think of taking those precautions? Did I know about it vaguely? I had a vague feeling that some such thing might happen. That's why when Ranganadha Rao brought the school money I deposited it in the bank on Saturday. I gave Suguna a thousand rupees. I put five thousand in my purse and packed it in my suitcase. That's why they couldn't get hold of it.

Two nights ago, Venkata Chalapati, Sri Ram and Madan came to my father's aid, called the police on the phone and did whatever was needed. And they sent a message to us in Tirupati, where we had gone on a pilgrimage.

Here I must report especially on the agitation that was stirred up in my mind. In the middle of the night of Saturday the 12th, while we were soundly asleep in cottage No. 83A of the ATC, Swami sent a message through a policeman. I was woken up; I went out and phoned. Prahlad and Swami told me about the burglary back home. When they finished, I thought for a moment that my heart had stopped. When I asked Venkata Chalapati anxiously what all they had stolen, he reported briefly that it didn't look like they had touched the steel cabinet. I was relieved. From what he said it seemed like all the major items were in their places. I didn't disclose the news to Suguna thinking that we probably hadn't lost much. All five of us got up early Sunday morning, washed, went to the after-worship *darshan* and had the *darshan* of the image of Venkateswara to our heart's content. There was a humungous crowd. Everything went according to schedule. By 6 a.m., we left for the foothills in the car.

Ever since I learned about the Saturday night burglary, my mind has become agitated. I worried about what they had stolen, how they might have strewn things around the house and what losses I might have incurred.

I remember having written on the topic of burglary before, especially regarding UG's opinions on this. He does not just have opinions; his feelings on the matter show even in the ways he acts.

As a matter of fact, he doesn't like us to use the word "stealing". "If you won't let me take what I want, then I will trick you and take it in my own way. If you then call my action stealing, I won't object," – that has been his disposition ever since he was young.

"Steal, but don't get caught," is one of UG's maxims. It's a truth which he has understood and applied in his life literally.

That night I was lying sleeplessly in bed in the cottage room thinking: "Don't I know the song, 'Do I live forever? How long will I live? None of these [*things and people*] will come with me when I die?' Still, why this attachment saying 'These things are mine; I own them'? What's the problem if I don't possess them? Poor fellows, if they take whatever they need, why do I get agitated? I wonder why I didn't think at that time of the Bible sentence which UG quotes, 'The Lord hath given, and the Lord hath taken away; blessed be the name of the Lord'!" I thought of UG for a while and lay in bed.

Thoughts: What might the police be doing around the house? The police and the street dogs were probably making a lot of noise. Why did this happen? Why did such a calamity occur right when we had gone to the Hill for the *darshan*? My mind was searching for a cause-and-effect connection.

I was walking around appearing confident, without yet revealing the news to Suguna and the others. But I wasn't at peace. To come to such a settled state as "Whatever I've lost, I've lost; what do I care about it?" it took me some time. "I have this anxiety, pain and disturbance only if I think those things are mine. If this body itself is not mine, what do I care about these other things?" The mind simmered and began to calm down. I only form dependence on or bonds with those things which I think are mine. The day is nearing when I have to take leave from this world. I know that the world will be perfect even without me. But still, what's the meaning of such a thing happening on the same day that we undertook a trip to Tirupati?

"Our days are not good. That's why everyone in the household is suffering from fever, and the burglary and such other calamities are taking place," said Suguna when I reported to her about the incident.

"So what if your things are gone? If the burglars take away unnecessary things, then your burden is reduced. If they take the things you needed, then you can buy new ones. Where's the loss in this?" asks UG.

Some years ago, when Archana was sad because someone had stolen her old sandals, UG promptly said, "Why are you so sorry that you have lost some old shoes? You must be glad that you will be getting new ones." How true! Archana didn't regret their loss very much.

I recalled all those things and reconciled myself. Still, the inner disturbance has not gone away completely. I wasn't at peace until I came home and ran an inventory.

* * *

The more I look the more I am amazed at how everyone is gripped by a desire for security. Security can take different shapes, depending on the mentality of the person. To a family man, security is having a family; and to the renunciate, security is in trying to save the world. If you look into these two deeply, they are based on the same desire. The family man reveres the monk; he treats him with respect. He worships him because he thinks that he has conquered his selfishness and is striving to help others. The monk too falls into the same deception. His pride is to think that he is moving away from personal problems and desires and is striving for the welfare of mankind. But, however much he tries to get rid of his pride, however much he broadens his mind with the idea of giving, he will not be completely free of the idea that he is superior to the family man. The family man gains security with the idea that he is doing good for many people. "This is going well; I must progress in this fashion; I must improve," that's what you need to feel continually for your sense of security. It is to feel secure that we worship, meditate, do charity, feed the poor and make pilgrimages. While we are doing all these things, we tell ourselves, "I am doing these things. I am dedicating these actions to God and am acting disinterestedly." Through such thinking our sense of security gains strength.

I have many thoughts about this. Can I write them all down this morning? This writing, as a matter of fact, is my security, my main support. I feel I am alive when I write.

My eyes are closing. It must be from the Horlicks I drank.

* * *

The news of the burglary spread all around by word of mouth. Some phoned and expressed their sympathy. Some others visited us to console us. Although we had not informed them, many people got to know of it anyway. It's becoming impossible to convince those who have come to comfort us that we haven't lost much, that we've only lost, as far as we know, a couple of things, and that we are not experiencing any hardship from losing them. "Is that so? You haven't lost anything of value? All your money and jewelry are safe? They didn't steal them?" they ask as though they can't believe me. Many seemed disappointed that the burglars didn't bother with the steel cabinet. Some seemed to be almost mad that after successfully breaking the locks and doors and entering, the burglars had not ransacked the whole house.

What were the burglars expecting to take? Why did those brave people who put forth so much effort in daring to break in run away with almost empty hands? I don't understand that. I think that they were probably looking for some cash or gold. They couldn't find anything of value in the wooden cabinet. The steel cabinet was not open. It was locked. And they might have hesitated to open it. They didn't seem to want just anything that was readily at hand. And all they could find was the tape recorder. They didn't get mad that they couldn't find what they wanted and break or destroy things. They seem pretty honourable, as thieves go.

Archana said yesterday, "Whoever they are, if I see them, I would like to interview them: 'How did you like our house? Whose room did you like best? What did you want the most when you saw our things here? What are your tastes? Didn't you have enough time to take more? Why did you stop in the middle and leave? You didn't like the things in our house?'" She said she would have liked to ask them such questions.

They seem to be gentlemen. I feel that they came to warn us to guard our house more carefully. Yesterday, after reviewing this whole affair at her leisure, Suguna became terrified. "Suppose something had happened, something that I can't imagine had happened...," she worried.

* * *

The consciousness of "I" is implanted deeply...

June 16, 1999, Wednesday

It has become a habit of mine to think that whatever happens is ultimately for our own good, that the final outcome will eventually be beneficial. With the events that had occurred last Saturday still fresh in our minds, Suguna and I have been consoling ourselves in different ways: that some force caused all this for our own good; that because such an event was unavoidable, as the proverb says, "whereas the head should have gone [*been beheaded*], only the turban was lost"; that this warning will lead us to take more precautions so that such calamities might not happen again; that there is a Force that has been constantly looking after our welfare; and that the few things that were lost were a good riddance.

I can only laugh at our foolishness. Yesterday evening I told Major, "I believe that an omnipresent Force is protecting us constantly and looking after our welfare."

"Yes, good, keep to that belief," he said laughing. I heard sarcasm in that laughter. The sarcasm indicated his thinking that after all these years of company with UG I hadn't gotten rid of my old beliefs.

Then should I not believe? I certainly do believe. The Lord of all, the Omnipresent is not only in me and but is everywhere and is maintaining the difference between Him and me. As long as I have a consciousness of myself, God exists for me. He deludes me into believing that He is sometimes with me and sometimes other than me, sometimes near me and sometimes far away.

This consciousness of "I" is implanted so deeply and intensely that I no longer think that the belief in it will ever go away even if my body perishes. I think it will continue in some form or other. If it not only creates my existence and maintains it by even continuing in my sleep and dreams, where is the guarantee that it won't remain even after my death? Such is my rational thinking.

Still, I forget that events don't always conform to that rational order. When something happens, I try to connect its antecedents and consequents rationally as causes and effects – isn't this falling into an illusion? I am inevitably reminded of the song in the film *Vemana*: "Don't fall into delusion, oh, my mind!" Since recalling that song, movie dialogues and scenes have been running past my eyes. Nagayya's unique and amazing acting comes alive before my eyes. My head is full of these thoughts. Will they ever stop?

* * *

A Memento for the Barber

June 17, 1999, Thursday

UG has a different influence on each person. Even those who meet him casually cannot forget him. They frequently recall their time with him. When UG arrived this time, he said he had to go a barber. Normally he goes to the hairdresser in the Holiday Inn (now La Meridian Hotel). He sheds a hundred rupees there for a haircut. UG remunerates the barber well. I don't even have to mention how he rewards the tailor.

"We are lucky to find people to work for us. It's not enough to pay them exactly; you must satisfy and gratify them grandly. We must pay them much more than what is due for their service," is UG's policy. He lives that way.

For some reason, UG was reluctant to go that far for a haircut this time. When I suggested that there is a barber shop near our house and I could call that barber, UG agreed. The time then was past 12 noon, almost 1 p.m. I went and interrupting the lunch the barber was about to eat, brought him to our home. He gave UG a nice haircut, making him sit in the portico in a chair. Once his hair was cut, UG gave him a 50-rupee bill with his own hands. I can't even remember the barber's name. He saluted UG very happily and left.

The other day, I went over to his shop for a haircut. As soon as he saw me he asked, "Did that gentleman leave, sir? When will he come again?" Then, the entire time that he was cutting my hair, he only spoke of UG and asked questions about him. With just one meeting, he had realised that UG was an extraordinary man. "Where can we meet such people? How fortunate I was to give him a haircut! It must be because of my merit from a previous life. I will never spend the Rs.50 he has given me. I have framed the bill and will preserve it," he said showing me the 50-rupee bill in a frame. He requested, "Please give me a picture of him, sir." I promised I would, surely. I am thinking of hand delivering a photo of UG to him. I saw a great veneration and joy in him as though he had seen God Himself. He doesn't care about what UG says or what sort of things he talks about. Just to see him is enough for him. It's enough to have the pleasure of cutting his hair. Remembering UG talking to him so kindly and waving a reassuring hand at him when he left, the barber was overjoyed as though he had attained a high spiritual state.

* * *

"What is your relationship to these things?"

June 25, 1999, Friday

As it was an auspicious day yesterday there were all sorts of religious functions going on everywhere. We discovered that someone had stolen a stereo tape player from my Maruti car, which was parked under the tree in front of our home, by opening its small window. Prahlad was parking his scooter outside the gate in the morning around 6 a.m. when he hollered, "Uncle, come out here, you must see for yourself!" I thought something terrible had happened and my heart beat fast. The back door of the car was open. Strewn on the front seat were pieces of tape, screws and some of the parts that had been taken apart. The thief had skilfully removed the player in order to take it. I was furious when I learned about the theft. Following Venkata Chalapati's advice, I reported the theft to the police. I called a mechanic from the Maruti Garage and got the window as well as the loose parts reconnected. I gave him Rs. 20 for the work he did. I phoned Suguna and told her about the theft from the car. I hardly went out all day. I stayed home and corrected an e-mail problem on the computer with the help of Satyam's tech support. In the evening, Chalapati and I gave a statement to Santa Raj, the inspector, in the police station. He assured us that he would make out the FIR [*report*] tomorrow. Chalapati also signed the report as a witness. I didn't go to the office in the evening. And I didn't go to the School either. I didn't move out of the house except for going to the police station. Archana came home early. Prahlad promised to come early, but came around 10 p.m.

* * *

I have been upset about the theft yesterday, the second within two weeks, and about losing the tape player in the car. Yesterday, while I sat alone at home, I had all sorts of fears running in my mind. I would look out if I heard any sound. How to live? How to be secure? I was afraid that the "expert" who could steal so quietly and mercilessly from a car which was parked right in front of the owner's house, knowing well that there were people in the house, could indeed do anything. What has happened to my goodwill towards all living things? Where did my detachment, which presumably regards even my own body as alien, hide? Why am I so confused when a small gadget, which I thought was mine, is gone? What would I do if the car itself is stolen? What would I do if my whole house is robbed? Why do I have so much confusion?

I asked myself: "What is the relationship between you and these things? Do all these things really exist? There! Your "philosophy" is what irritates me! None of these exist? You say that they don't exist? Then, why were you so sad all day yesterday? What was that agitation inside you? Why were you so absent-minded as to let the rice in the cooker get burnt? Why is your stomach still upset? What indeed did you lose that belonged to you? Why are you so afraid that you feel you must lock your house? What will happen to you when the time comes for you to leave this world? If you are so perturbed by such a small theft, when the moment comes when you are fated to die and are about to exit this world for good, how much bigger will the storm be that will be raised in your mind? You have been so proud that nothing bothers you and you are not enamoured by anything. Yet, if some such small thing, something which is not of everyday use to you, is gone, why are you so sad? It has taken you so long to settle down after this."

Even Suguna didn't mention the theft to anyone. Nonetheless, she too must have been disturbed. In all that confusion, the milk boiled over. It's not good enough for me to console myself saying, "What's not ours won't remain with us. If we deserve it, we will have it, or else, we won't." Why should there be so much agitation in my mind in the first place? After learning so many things and hearing so much philosophy, after being associated with UG for so many years and boasting that I am ready even to die, why should I become dejected with such a trifle? "However much you have learned, however much you have seen...," [*the first line of a song by Tyagaraja*] is this, indeed, your final destiny? Are you truly not afraid of death? Are you ready to say goodbye to the world?

I didn't notice any fear in the faces of those criminals who had been caught and held in the police station. On the contrary, they appeared quite fearless. The police will beat them. Still, they won't care. One criminal tried to grab the feet of the inspector, confessing his guilt. But the inspector pounded him on his back and kicked him. Then the inspector turned toward us and talked as if he was a peaceful person. Is he some kind of an enlightened man? Is there any possibility of an iota of humaneness remaining in these people who spend year after year, day in and day out, with thieves like this?

Is there truly such thing as humaneness? It's easy to talk about humane qualities as long as everything goes smoothly as expected. It's when things go wrong that the humane quality must stir within you. When circumstances go awry, when your existence is about to disappear, when terrible things happen, you become a totally selfish person. Selflessness, compassion, pity, empathy, altruism, mercy — they all will end up as mere words. You will sit like a frozen rock.

What's the difference between you and those miserable people, those thieves who toil day in and day out to fill their bellies? To add to it, you complain about them to the police? Is this how cultured you are? Is your culture merely to preach morals to others, so long as those morals don't apply to you? Is this what you have learned after being educated for so many years, after suffering a few shocks in life and striving for higher states? The song Nagayya sang in the cremation ground holding a skull in his hand – "Is this all? Is this all there is to life in the end?" comes to mind. In the movie *Vemana*, Vemana [*played by Nagayya*] wails: "Must one finally mingle in the dust, after wearing various garbs ever since the time of birth, and living through childhood, youth, adulthood and old age? What is the secret of death? What is the aim of life?" Sadasiva [*God*], who appears in the form of his guru, asks Vemana a counter question, "Do you think that there is even any ultimate meaning at all to life, my son?"

* * *

"Why do you worry?"

July 27, 1999, Sunday

I was sad today even before I got up from bed. My mind is getting knotted up again. Yesterday, I saw a poster, on the wall of Sudha Clinic, which said, "Why do you worry?" It said reassuringly, "50 per cent of your worries do not come to pass." We can say even a higher percentage don't. Still the mind won't quit its worrying. Maybe it's a human characteristic to elaborate on the calamities that might yet come and the dangers that might pounce on us, thus depriving ourselves of any joy that exists in this moment, reducing it to a moon shining through a thick jungle.

Now, right at this moment, while I am writing this, what do I lack? No, these worries and thoughts just won't stop. They race in my head like express trains. Nevertheless, I haven't yet lost the confidence that I can stop them. That's why I make all this effort. If I keep writing like this, I may be able to reduce their impact somewhat.

I have another thought as to what the connection is between my thoughts and myself. When the anxieties become more intense, my heart palpitates and my mouth becomes dry. The bodily situation becomes similar to one of facing a danger. My stomach gets upset.

I feel like I have to go to the bathroom. I can't focus on anything. Meaningless fears overwhelm me. In that situation, I feel like I lack strength and that I might fall flat on the floor.

Why do things happen like this? Is it because I lack the courage to face circumstances? Why this dread of danger? The root cause of all these fears is the worry that whatever we have will be lost. So what? Will I carry all that with me when the time to depart nears? Still the mind sticks to worries like glue.

The doctors' announcing that Raghavendra Rao's health has been deteriorating is the main reason why I was grabbed by these fears yesterday. Other worries in the background include wondering about the precautions I had taken regarding the house and the money I have been spending on them, and the thought that "our times are not right." Today, ever since I got up, I have had a vague fear that some danger might be in store for today.

I don't think this fear creeps in from outside. I have made all possible effort, indeed, to escape from it. I lament, wondering "Is there a saviour who says 'I am here, I'll be your support and I will shoulder all your burdens and responsibilities,' or is there not?"

Then what is all this confusion? If you have true faith in the Lord at all, then why do you have these fears? If you have submitted everything to the Lord, then what do you care what happens? When will I be released from these fears? Maybe the yearning to be released from them is the main cause of them.

Everything is doubtful. I cannot stay with any single thought. Whatever I know is superficial; I have no strong and deep faith in anything; I have no confidence in anything. How fortunate is the fellow who can dump all his burdens on a stone God with a coconut and a salute and walk away washing his hands of them!

Just now, as I was writing this and worrying at the same time about the milk boiling over, I heard the sound of the milk beginning to boil over. By the time I rushed there, the milk had boiled over. But the mind doesn't stop regretting the incident. It gets hurt. It feels that the milk belongs to it and is dear to it.

That's how the mind is. It concocts a thousand fears. With its wild imagination it concocts so many dangers. It doesn't let you breathe. Holding on to a blind belief that there is definitely a way to get out of this is what makes me write like this. Why should I get out? What do I lose if I keep these worries, fears and anxieties? Why am I concerned about them? It's easy to write about this. But it should be experienced, right? But who should? Who will miss you if you are indeed totally destroyed? You? You need release? But from what?

"I know what happiness is not..."

Last night everything was fixed: the gate was repaired and iron doors with a metal frame were installed upstairs in the back of the house. The car is now parked inside the compound and is resting. The sofa is moved to the balcony upstairs. Everything looks strange because of the changes. The car parked in the portico looks strange. How have all these changes come to be? Why should I writhe in pain because some things were lost in the burglaries? I have been wondering about why Julie suffers even when she has a lot of money and could live as she wants. But then how am *I* any different?

"Why can't man be happy? How is it that he is unable to clean the filth of his own [*mind*]" contemplates Chalam in *Sudha*? "Why does man want to be permanently happy in the first place?" contemplates UG. The elders bless us saying, "May you be happy!" But what is happiness? Where do we find happiness? How did man come to strive for happiness? No one can answer these three questions. I truly don't know. I know what happiness is not. I know where it is not. And I know there is striving for it.

* * *

"Do you think that there is any ultimate meaning, my son?"

June 28, 1999

As soon as I got up in the morning today Suguna mentioned that she had had a nightmare that UG had died and that she had kept crying in the dream. I used to feel that I couldn't imagine a world in which there was no UG. UG was part of my very existence once upon a time. Now, does UG exist? Where is he except in your mind? I just believe he exists. I just think. If this world doesn't exist, where am I? Where indeed am I? All other thoughts are based on the idea of "I am" like the warp and woof of a huge woven edifice. If that piece, that little piece called "I am" is not there, the whole edifice will collapse. Even the thought "I don't exist" is part of the thought of "I am." If I am not there how am I conscious that "I am"? When there is no way of knowing it, how could one determine whether I am or I am not?

Last night I was watching the movie *Vemana* and making a video copy of it till midnight. It took a couple of hours. No matter how many times I watch it, I don't get tired of it. I feel there is a whole philosophy implied in the dialogue between Siva Yogi and Vemana. When Vemana says, "I am unable to find the ultimate meaning of life, Swami," Siva Yogi asks him the counter question, "Do you think that there is any ultimate meaning, my son?" A UG-like trend of thought is evident in that answer. There is truth in Sharmila's saying that UG was Vemana Yogi in a previous life.

Vemana's struggle is only to find what death is. When Jyoti [*the name of his niece; also, lit. 'light'*] was extinguished, his world becomes empty. On the other hand, his previous infatuation with a courtesan evaporates when he finds out her true colours. Declaring, "Abhirama, everyone in this world is a son of the slave of him who has gold," he launches his effort to make gold through alchemy. He achieves that goal. But the heaven Vemana imagined collapses with the untimely death of Jyoti. Everything becomes hollow. He loses his will to live. As he does not believe in anything, his life then becomes a rudderless ship.

Finally, through the teaching of Siva Yogi he understands his true nature. "You are not concerned with what happens. Your true nature is not what you imagine. You stay where you are from moment to moment," God teaches Vemana, appearing to him in the form of Siva Yogi. Vemana becomes a yogi. He learns of the union with the entire animate and inanimate worlds, the truth beyond experience, without his being aware of it. Finally, as his final message to Abhirama, he says, "He who learns of where we come from and where we go will becomes liberated," and goes into the interior of a cave to lie down to die.

The movie is truly a work of art. No matter how many times you watch it, you won't get tired of it. *Malliswari* is also such a movie. It was produced some 50 years ago. It still pleases people like me.

* * *

Essential UG

Dakshinamurti and I were standing on the stairs to the second floor discussing the philosophical teaching of the movie *Vemana*. We wondered how the writer had come to have such an outlook. A statement like "As long as you have the notion that you are separate from this creation, your anxiety is inevitable, my son," doesn't seem to be based merely on a philosophical principle. I feel that the whole essence of UG's teaching is imbedded in that sentence. "You are not separate from what is happening. All your sorrows result from that feeling of difference you have." Then who has this anxiety? Who has the expectations? Who has the sorrow? Who has discord in life? Who is there to recognize? This truth cannot remain a mere principle but must operate in day-to-day experience.

* * *

Spirits and Satyanarayana

July 5, 1999, Monday

... It seems that there is no culture in the world that doesn't have some belief in ghosts and spirits. We think that Western nations are more scientifically oriented, but their interest in supernatural experiences is even greater than ours. When Major returned the book he had borrowed from Satyanarayana, we talked about these things. Satyanarayana described his experiences regarding his mother. I felt that I should preserve them in writing.

Satyanarayana's mother was psychic. She used to have extrasensory experiences. She was an illiterate; she was a common middleclass housewife and mother of many children. Her husband didn't stay home much. Gripped by his spiritual craze, he often wandered around the country, served the *sadhus* he met in his travels, returning home only when he felt like it. His dead sister apparently used to appear to Satyaranarayana's mother. She used to possess her sometimes. At those times his mother would become ravenously hungry. The poor lady apparently would beg for *vadais* and *payasam* and eat huge amounts of food. When she was released from the possession, she would become normal.

Satyanarayana told me that he felt that the difference between

Western spirits and these spirits is that in those countries, the spirits mostly seem to thirst for blood and hunger for sex, while in this country, they like to eat dishes that they are fond of. He went on to say that of the 12 children his mother had borne, eight became victims to the spirit. His mother had with her own hands laid the baby that was born before Satyanarayana on live charcoal with benzoin sprinkled on it. Despite her state of possessed frenzy, however, she heard the baby's scream, returned to her senses and quickly pulled the baby off the fire. A few days later the baby died. Satyanarayana told me that it was the spirit that was the cause of this happening. His mother used to see the spirit directly. She could see her clearly and talk to her just as she could see everyone else. At times she played a game of shells with her.

One time, her sister came to visit her. Those were the days when Satyanarayana was still a baby. While her sister sat near the cradle, rocking it, the spirit came. Normally, the spirit would take the baby into her lap and then leave after playing with it for a while. But the mother did not like the spirit coming and picking up the baby; but she didn't dare oppose the spirit. That day, the spirit didn't come inside the house. She stayed outside and asked the mother to place the baby in her arms. When the mother asked her to come in and get the baby herself, she replied, "Your sister is standing in the way. I can't come in." Then it occurred to his mother that it would be safer for her child to be raised by her sister. That same day, she made her sister the ward of her child. That's how Satyanarayana survived.

In her final days, three days before she died, she called Satyanarayana to come from his office and told him, "Today I am still in a condition to be able to speak to you. By tomorrow I won't have this sort of consciousness. You must take on the responsibility of your sister's marriage. Even if the groom is a beggar, you must give her in wedlock to someone and make her a married woman. After that, her fate will take care of her life." Exactly on that day, a matchmaker came looking for a bride and his sister's marriage was arranged.

Satyanarayana's sister's life is similar to that of Goda Devi. Just as it happens in the mythologies, the couple's astrological signs and horoscope were of the same kind. Satyanarayana read in some book about a "propitiation" [*a ritual to counteract the evil effects of planets*] and arranged for it at his sister's wedding. The auspicious moment of the wedding approached soon. Satyanarayana had his mother in his mind till the last moment.

While still talking to everyone lucidly, she said, "Your father is beckoning me." When Satyanarayana showed her the photos of his father and asked her if she could tell the name of the person in them, she would not. When he pressed her, she joined her two hands and recited the "*Chandrasekhara Ashtakam*". His father's name was Chandrasekharayya.

Satyanarayana asked his mother many questions regarding the sighting of these spirits. "You ask me so many questions because you don't believe. But how can I brush off my own experience?" she would reply. Satyanarayana had no way of challenging what she said.

"Do you believe in all these things?" Major asked him. I can't remember what Satyanarayana's answer was. But he does believe. Whatever terms one uses, terms such as "vibrations" and 'spirits', everyone has gone through some extrasensory experience. UG too has spoken of such things and of the incidents that had happened to him.

When someone once asked him, "Then isn't "death" the end? Will there be something remaining after that?" "I don't know what remains, but find out what there is now," he replied. If you know what there is now, then you will understand what will remain tomorrow. We don't even know that. Just words, a show of words – we don't know anything more. If there is something, does it mean that it's something separate from "me"? The "I' is just a memory. Yet, there is nothing separate and beyond it. There is no way to know whether that memory will survive or will perish with the body. To know is to remember. There is nothing beyond memory. Intelligence is also memory. It must shine as the light of experience. It should fill with light. Till then, doubts will not subside. This is what I discussed with Major and Venkata Chalapati last evening.

The consciousness of myself, and the intelligence that says, "I am", exist separately. But I don't understand UG when he says that the 'you" is a mere fear.

"Why this futile yearning to bring into experience what is beyond experience?" asks UG. That's the source of man's restlessness. Why can't he achieve that state of mind which can accept whatever happens without question? 'Achieve" doesn't mean that you have to do anything. Nevertheless, I can't believe that it will happen without my doing something. If such a state occurs, then all these questions will stop. This duality will disappear. But that unity is not the unity that the Vedantins teach. It's not imagining in your head, "One, without a second," and living a solitary life or living in caves or on mountain peaks or in jungles. That unity will remain the simplest mystery which will never be known. No one can know or explain it.

* * *

The Documentary Produced by BBC

Last night, Mahesh phoned. Apparently some BBC people met Mahesh yesterday and asked his permission to produce a documentary. They are trying to depict the prominent influences in the lives of celebrities. Mahesh said to me, "What other influence has there been on me except UG's? So, the BBC crew and I are coming to Bangalore on the 15th. Exactly twenty years ago, in "Sastri Sadan" in West Anjaneya Street, a new life of mine began. 'When you look back, you will know that this day is an important day in your life, Mahesh! Go and mould your life and your future in a grand fashion,' UG said, patting me on the shoulder and seeing me off. I have never looked back since that day," said Mahesh.

What a state he was in twenty years ago! That was when Mahesh had broken up with Parveen. He didn't have any credible position in the movie field. Every film he had produced was a flop. They nicknamed him "flop director". Since that day, he has toiled and built his career gradually. He never turned away from UG's influence. This year he is quitting his work as a film director. "We are coming to shoot a documentary on that street, the temple premises, the house "Sastri Sadan" – all those places which stood as silent witnesses," continued Mahesh. He said they would shoot Major's Farm House also. I must tell him to include "Poorna Kuti" as well. If we need to, we can get permission to enter it that day from Mr. Narayana Dasu. On the phone Mahesh recalled UG's previous warning "Let the BBC people come to you first; don't rush into it."

* * *

July 17, 1999 (Saturday)

Yesterday, I got ready early in the morning. Mahesh brought his car exactly at 5 a.m. Fifteen minutes later, Mahesh and I were having coffee in the West End Hotel. From there we went to MG Road with the BBC crew. They set up a camera tripod in the middle of the road in front of Gangaram's. The sky was heavily overcast. The BBC people travelled from Delhi especially to film the documentary. One of them was a young lady called Nandini. The photographer was Sankar Raman. They both live in Bombay now. Raman is a South Indian. When Suguna made *dosais* and served them, he ate about six or seven of them with gusto. "When I eat these *dosais*, I am reminded of the *dosais* my mother used to make, Auntie," he complimented. Nandini is a Maharashtrian. Her grandfather was a lieutenant colonel in the army. As soon as she mentioned her grandfather's name, it caused a whole history to spill from Dakshinamurti's encyclopaedic memory. I can't remember the name of that colonel, try as I might. I don't know how Major can remember all that. It's amazing. While watching a documentary on Budapest on the Discovery Channel, Major narrated the whole story of that city. When I asked him, "How do you know all this?" he told me that he had read about it in the newspapers when he was young. There is a river which connects the two cities of Buda and Pest. The two cities together are now called Budapest. It's the capital of Hungary. How many things he knows like this! He has a great memory. He has the ability to recite verbatim anything even after many years.

It was two days ago when Mahesh had helped the BBC crew film "Sastri Sadan" on West Anjaneya Temple Street. They filmed the scenes of Mahesh pushing the calling bell, my opening the door, coming out and talking to him and so on. Meanwhile, many girls who were on the way to their school in BMS College gathered around Mahesh for his autograph. Then, around 2 p.m., we went to Vidyarthi Bhavan Restaurant.

Twenty years ago, in October 1979, Mahesh's new life was launched in West Anjaneya Temple Street. "Forget everything that has happened up till now. You must mould a new future, Mahesh. If you fail, I will never forgive you," UG said, putting him into an auto-rickshaw and bidding him goodbye. In that same spot, two days ago, Mahesh reminisced about UG's prophesy made twenty years ago, "When you look back, this day will seem to be historic to you."

What days they were! A new life started for me in the same house. Marriage with Suguna, setting up house, children being born, advancement in career – they all happened in "Sastri Sadan". How many memories there are surrounding this old house! "Man is a bundle of memories and nothing more," says UG. The life of an individual is nothing but remembering many things and living in the past. That's all.

Yesterday morning, when Mahesh and I were going to the Farm House in the Maruti car, Mahesh remarked "Yesterday, suddenly a question grabbed me, Babu," and he told me about it.

He had been sitting alone in his West End Hotel room. The BBC people had left by then. Mahesh thinks that the atmosphere in that hotel is like nowhere else in the country. There is a dense garden in the yard. Where you look, you see the greenery of the grand hundred-year-old trees. If you are looking from inside the room, you have the illusion of being in a jungle. You don't feel that you are in a hotel. The rooms are decorated quite tastefully. When you enter the street from the hotel, you are right in the central hub of the town. Wherever you want to go, it's only about twenty minutes by car. "Nowhere else can you find such convenience," remarked Mahesh.

Sitting in that West End Hotel room, Mahesh had been suddenly struck with doubt: "How do I know that this is the West End and that this is Bangalore; how am I able to know that a person called "I" exists?" He felt this not just as a set of thoughts or questions, but as a search which filled his whole existence. "How do I know?" That's right. How do I know that I am such and such and that all these things around here pertain to me?

* * *

Then Mahesh phoned last evening from Bombay. "Babu, Ajay Devgun in my movie, *Zakhm* got the Best Actor award. And there were two more awards. Altogether my last film got three national awards," he told me. I congratulated him happily. *Zakhm* is based on his mother's story. I haven't seen it yet. Isn't it remarkable that right at the same time that he has been reminiscing his life of twenty years ago in Bangalore, remembering about how UG's unique influence had resurrected his ruined life, that his current work of art has been awarded three national awards? What more could he be proud of? Mahesh's life is fulfilled. When UG said, "If you fail in life, I will never forgive you," as though he was rubbing salt into his wound, he had been a true inspiration for Mahesh's success.

Baba

September 14, 1999, Tuesday

This machine called the brain starts working as soon as I get up from bed in the morning. I think that the noise goes on even during my sleep. You just can't hear it from outside. It starts as soon as I wake up. From that moment, it goes on till I drop off to sleep at night. What can I do? When I look back, I realise I have been fighting this "noise" all my life — different kinds of noises, some which I like and some which are frightening — now especially the grinding noise of thoughts about the School. There is some ringing sound in my ears. If I listen to it inside my left ear I can hear it clearly. If I keep writing like this, I repeat each word within myself. Do I know this "I" which has taken such deep roots in me? Who is it that is anxious to know?

"There is only the Supreme Lord," said Jitendra Baba yesterday. We finished the Ganesha *puja* and went with Major to Baba's home in the afternoon at 4:00 p.m. in his car. "Have you ever worshipped Ganesha? Have you ever experienced Him?" I asked Baba. "Who is sitting by my side and holding my hand if not Ganesha?" replied Baba to me as I sat next to him. Suddenly, he started asking questions about the School. "I want to see your School. I like spending time with little kids," he said. Major said that he would bring him to my home at 11 a.m. on Wednesday to go there.

Baba speaks of "total surrender". He says that the Supreme Lord takes care of everything, of all the things he needs. He speaks as if God is closely watching whatever is happening to him. "Why bring the Supreme Lord into this?" was Major's question.

UG's state is also a state of total surrender; but in it there is no division between him and the Supreme Lord. UG doesn't know what's happening and to whom it's happening. The division arises at times in UG's consciousness. But then it disappears instantly. So, he has no need for the Supreme Lord. There is no person who weighs the good and the bad of what happens. That's the difference between UG's state and the state of surrender that Baba deliberately tries to stay in. "What business do I have to do with a God who is merciful only to those who pray to him? What about people like me who don't care about him?" asks UG mockingly. There is no "selectivity" there. UG's "decision" is God's command.

* * *

What is this writing for? Deliberately composing, collecting and selecting from past notes – for whose sake? Who will be the loser if I don't write? I will be. This is for my pleasure. What pleasure? For how long? Only as long as I write. There is a possibility that tomorrow someone might read and enjoy this if I at least write down the gossip about UG. But who is really interested in this empty talk?

"What do you want?"

September 21, 1999, Tuesday

"What do you want?" UG asks very pointedly. "What do you want?" is his *mantra*. To those who ask him, "What should I do, UG?" this is his counter question. True, what indeed do I want? What I am searching for? This is a more potent question than the question "Srinivasarao, what are you searching for?" in Sri Sri's *Mahaprasthanam*. There are ways of obtaining whatever I want. There are also problems in those ways, depending on what I want, because many other people may want the same thing. When we want "happiness", that narrow path becomes crowded. In that overcrowded place, whether you can get what you want depends on your relative strength. UG makes it quite simple. However, if you look into it in depth, what you want is not just one thing; you want a hundred thousand things. If those hundred thousand desires have to be satisfied, then there is a risk of there being a hundred thousand paths. Which way should I go? Just as the student who doesn't know which way to go [*the allusion is to a poem in Sri Sri's* Mahaprasthanam] – 'to see Norma Shearer in Roxy or…' — I have to put on a sorry face. Unless we are clear beforehand that we want such and such, just that one thing and only that, we will be in unnecessary trouble. We will go hither and thither, wasting our time, energy and the prime of our God-given life (*vayassu*).

What do I want – what one thing do I want; not what hundred thousand desires do I have? While yearning, why does my mind always swing incessantly like a clock pendulum, saying, "That... and I want that?" What is the one desire about which I can say "There is no question of having another; I want just this one thing," and stay put without wavering back and forth? Where is that flame in me which remains burning like a wildfire and is never extinguished? Have I been yearning for just that one thing for the past fifty years? I am unable to answer this one question after all these years. This moment I desire one thing, the next moment I desire another. I have been multiplying desires like this all these fifty years. I can't remember my first three or four years. But when I review these fifty years I have lived, I feel that it's not a life that I have lived. I must feel that way. After all, will I ever be able to get an answer to the question, "What do I want?" I wrote a poem 25 years ago, "What do you want...?" Has that question been pursuing me ever since, like the Brahma's missile? If just that one question completely possessed me, would I still be able to breathe, to keep my bearings or even think another thought? Would it let me?

* * *

How does the desire for a particular thing arise in the first place? Is it only because someone pounded it into my head that I should desire it? If the desire is not satisfied, what's lost now? And for whom is the loss? If I find an answer to the first question, so many other questions pop up. My logic poses all these questions, but where is there room for them if my whole existence is occupied by the first question? Where is the scope for another question? That indeed, is true, too. So, first, let there be an answer to that first question, namely, "What do I want?" Whatever answer I get, it seems like that's not it. I want something else. But I don't know what. When will I know? How long will it take for me to know? What else should I learn first in order to know that? I must be clear about what I want. What's the use of seeking someone else's help? Can I clear up the problem? Why can't I? Is it really clear to me that all other questions are secondary compared to this?

* * *

My mind is agitated...

September 22, 1999, Wednesday

Julie called yesterday. Apparently, when UG recently talked to Guha, Lakshmi and her, he had asked her to convey a stern warning to me: "Tell Chandrasekhar that I won't come to India until he gets all the videos, audios and photos into some shape." How should I preserve them and yet make them accessible to everyone? Suppose I give them to some institution? Will they use them properly? I must consult the people at the Indian Institute of Culture and find out. Can they preserve them all and make them accessible to the public? Can they find the money to do it? All these are questions. Or else, if something is not done about them, they will all perish. Then they will be utterly useless.

* * *

My mind is agitated. Even when I get out of bed in the morning, it's not quiet. The source of all this anxiety is to think that I am doing everything: all the things that need to be done in the future, those things that have already been done and the things I am now doing. All these things will go on; will they stop just because I die? Some people around me may face some problems at first. Then things will go on as usual.

* * *

"Mahesh should have no mission at all..."

September 20th was Mahesh's birthday. I called yesterday morning and wished him a belated "Happy Birthday." Apparently, on that day, Tanuja asked UG, "Today is Mahesh's birthday. What should his mission be from now on?" UG replied at once without hesitation, "He should have no mission at all. He should be free." Mahesh has completed 50 years. He told me he is 51. So many of us have gotten into our fifties. Even Suguna will be 50 next January. The questions have not gone yet: I have only accumulated more of them and I am making no attempt to get rid of them. I must first distance myself from the illusory notions that "I" am doing, that things happen because of me and that I am the agent and the enjoyer. Burdens only get heavier because of such notions. It's some sort of false living. What does really happen because of me? If I had a free bowel movement for the last couple of days, is it due to my greatness or to the effect of the fenugreek seeds I have eaten to induce it?

* * *

Tips for filmmaking...

Twenty years ago, Mahesh Bhatt was called a "flop director" in the movie world. Ten years later, everyone in Bollywood started thinking of him as "Machine Bhatt". His unhindered industriousness, his discipline of working 18 hours a day without rest, paved the way to his success. It was perhaps around 1979–80 that UG had taken Mahesh along with all of us to the Telugu movie, *Maro Charitra*, in Alankar Theatre. Balachander directed the movie in which Kamal Hasan acted. I think UG gave Mahesh many tips by means of discussing that movie. "The ending is very depressing," said UG, referring to the tragic ending of that movie. "You have to play on the sentiments of the people. If the audience leaves the theatre with a feeling of wanting to watch the movie a second time, your film is a success. Don't bother about the reviews that the film critics write in the newspapers and magazines. It's the *riksha-walah* or the taxi-*walah* who decides the fate of your film," he told Mahesh that day. He still says the same thing. Now he is asking Mahesh to quit directing movies. He says he has done enough of that; he must start new things.

* * *

"What can I do as an individual?..."

September 23, 1999, Thursday

We got the news that the power would be cut off every day at 6 p.m. starting yesterday. We won't have power for two hours. Even now, the lights are dim because the voltage is very low. If there is no power, we will have trouble getting drinking water. Why did they have to impose this power-cut even when there is so much rainfall throughout the country? Only the government knows the answer to this. It may be an election strategy. To make it convenient to pump more water to their farmer friends, they cut off the power here in the cities. That's how it is in this country. They can't do anything right. That's why UG speaks about this country so disapprovingly. There is no awareness in people. They only indulge themselves in the *karma* doctrine, sighing to themselves, "This is my *karma*; it has been fated this way." They won't pick up their energy and fight for their rights or toss their useless government onto a garbage heap.

What can I do as an individual? Do I have any power? What's the use of thinking unnecessarily about these things except to ruin my mental peace? Do I have the confidence and perseverance to achieve what I want? Am I so important? In the first place, what is the source of all these problems? Is the power-cut cutting me up or am I making a mountain out of a mole hill? What's the big loss if I don't have the power for a few hours? Am I being cowardly or wise to think in this manner? Why should I spoil my mental peace by worrying about things that are beyond my control? But, in the first place, why should I hanker for having a mind always content and happy? What does it matter if it's in turmoil or if it radiates beauty? What do I care?

The clock just struck seven. The power is out. I brought in the emergency lamp from the kitchen and am continuing my writing. Where then is the problem now?

* * *

Yesterday, I discussed video technology at length with Salini and Kumar, about how it would be possible to transcribe the videotapes onto CDs. If I can transcribe an hour's tape onto a CD first, I can think about the rest later. I should get them to do it before the end of this month.

* * *

UG's words from *What am I Saying*?

September 27, 1999, Monday

Suguna Krishnamurti arrived around 5:30 in the evening in her new car, an Omni, along with two of her friends. We all watched the video, *What am I Saying?* for an hour. UG may not know what he said in it, but his words are echoing in my head.

1. "We are all just puppets in the hands of nature. We don't have any free will. Where is that freewill you are talking about?" he says.

2. In another place he says, "Man is the moulder of his own future and architect of his own destiny." How are the above two statements compatible with each other? That's something to think about. But just as I was thinking about this, another bomb exploded.

3. "Through thinking you cannot understand a thing." My God! Then what does it mean to think? What does UG mean when he says that we cannot achieve anything, understand anything, through thinking? Oh God, explain what you mean! Again, thinking is the only rescue. I am reminded of Tyagaraja's song, "*Yochanaa, kamala lochanaa...*"

4. UG says again, explaining himself: "When I say "thinking", I don't mean the instinctive thinking like that of the animals which do some kind of thinking. The dog knows its master; it knows its way home. I don't mean that kind of thinking..." That means he is not talking about the things we do without thinking. They too arise out of some kind of thinking. If UG is not talking about that sort of thinking in us, then what sort of thinking *does* he mean?

5. "...any thinking other than that used for the survival of the organism. Thinking is only to change yourself from something to something other than what you are. Animals are not interested in changing themselves. This [*interest*] is put in us by the society or culture. That is responsible for thinking. Why do you want to change? To achieve something." The attempt to change myself, to get something, to achieve something, and the urges in me, the "I" —depend upon the society and culture I am born in and raised in. Thoughts arise on the basis of how I have been brainwashed.

6. "I don't have any thoughts other than those of my basic needs of food, clothing and shelter. I don't have any other questions. How come you all seem to have so many questions?" he asks. So many questions — Is there rebirth? What is the meaning of life? Does God exist? Are there other worlds? — Whence do all these questions arise? UG says he has no such questions. What happened to them?

7. "All these questions are born out of the answers you already have; you have the answers. They all have given you the answers. Why are you still asking the same questions? Obviously you are not satisfied with them [*those answers*]. If I give you any answer, you add this to the list you already have." True. There are heaps of answers within me. Why don't they satisfy me? How do I know about the bliss, the spiritual, the stillness of mind, the *samadhi*, the peace and so on that I desire? These are things that have been drummed into my ears. Who is the "I" that knows of them? Is my existence separate from that information?

8. "You're really not interested in my answer. You want to continue through that question; because the end of the question

is the end of you as you know yourself and experience yourself," says UG profoundly. "You cannot be interested in this. It will burn you. Don't play with this," he threatens. He does not "threaten", he warns. But the ending is not in my hands. These thoughts won't end. These fears won't go away. This distress, this anxiety won't subside. That's why UG says, "We are all puppets." We are all puppets in the hands of Fate. What to do? What should we do?

9. "Nothing. Live in misery and die in misery. That's the lot of humans," says UG and remains silent.

* * *

Thinking that "I am…"

September 29, 1999, Wednesday

It rained all of last night and the night before. It rained until this morning. There are only ten days left till the end of the month of Bhadrapada; after that come the Dasara holidays and the month of Aswayuja. There will be rains then, too. It has been raining for the last five or six days, since the full moon day. Before that, the sun was unexpectedly extremely hot.

UG has not called here yet or talked to anyone. No news of him.

My stomach is upset. There is ringing in my head. Or is it that my mind has dropped down into my stomach? This thing called the mind, its there if you think it is there; and it's not there, if you think it is not. Only the freedom to think it doesn't exist remains. If I think "it's not there" will it disappear? If I hide money in my wallet and think that I don't have a single penny, will the money disappear? It's easy to say that it's all in one's thinking, as if thinking and not thinking are both in our hands. "To me" [*mama* in Sanskrit] asks the priest to say to yourself. If I say that to myself, would all that [merit] transfer to my account? For instance, how come in the matter of the School, no matter how many times I have tried to think "not to me" [viz., "*I am not that*"], my worry keeps getting worse? But it has indeed become evident through all these forty years that telling myself as strongly as I can "This body and this mind are not mine. I am not concerned with them," is useless.

But there is a subtlety here. We don't know at what level that thinking must proceed. There is a strong hook-up somewhere in the head. That must be severed. The "I" and "mine" are strong anchors. As long as that anchor is there, no matter how much and how long you meditate telling yourself, "I am not this body; I am not this mind; I am not these thoughts," those anchors won't go away. When such a bond afflicts us, what good it is to say, "I must practice, I must practice?"

I wrote before in these notebooks that the notion of "I am" is the source of all problems. But what's the use of this writing? How have I benefited from the mere knowing of it? To think that "I am not" is not in my hands. There is no use even in thinking that "I am" or that "I am not." Then what to do? Why should I think that I must do something? "I can't do it; it's not in my hands" — as soon as the mechanism in my head grasps it, this hook-up is broken. If that wheel which goes around incessantly stops, all the worlds will stand still. I don't know if it will ever stop. But it's not in my power to stop it. It must go on turning like this. I must writhe in pain writing the same thing over and over again, thinking the same thing over and over again; tasting my own blood with relish; jumping with joy for being happy and patting my own back, thinking this is all due to my own greatness, my own intellect; and being disappointed, at the same time, when things I desire are not accomplished, crying my heart out when whatever I have is lost and grieving "Is there no saviour who can save me, no one dear to me? Oh God, won't you come?" till I die, till I breathe my last breath, till this body becomes a lifeless log. There is no other way. Not just UG, even if UG's "grandmother" came down, she can't be of any help. No one can help you. No one can give you a helping hand from any corner. Why do you keep pining for help? Why do you hope that the gates of heaven will open for you? Only your wasted effort will remain. Even if you teach yourself some sense like this, would your hopes and your yearning stop? They must go on as usual. The machine keeps turning in your head. And as long as the mill turns, the flour must fall from it. No one can stop it. Then why are you sad? What for? What does it matter if UG talks to you or not? Can UG stop this mill from turning? Then where would you be? And where would UG be?

* * *

Path of Righteousness

Q: UG, do you have any questions?

UG: I only want to ask you, "Why are you here? What do you want? What can I do for you?"

Q: How many people have you put on the path of righteousness?

UG: I have succeeded in taking away quite a lot of them from the path of righteousness and put them where they belonged. Whatever potential is there will surface because of being exposed to me. It's not spiritual. That doesn't exist. If you don't have any [*potential*], it's too bad.

* * *

"Dog is God..."

One day, Bhaskara Rao felt dizzy while he was walking in the middle of the road in the hot sun. He found some support that he could lean against. Standing in the sun, he saw in front of him a dog in a pitiable condition. It was still carrying on. Bhaskara Rao thought, "What's the difference between it and me?" Immediately, his dizziness was gone. His body recouped its energy. "From now on it is not "Dog", it's "God". It's my aim of life to attain its state," thought Bhaskara Rao. Major told me this.

* * *

The title *Sunakopanishad* [*Dog Upanishad*] is flashing in my head. Going on around it are the bits of all the things UG has said about dogs — the superiority of dogs, their spiritual superiority, how they run around wagging their tails. A beautiful essay is in the making. If I could put it down on paper... But why? What would I gain? Questioning myself like this makes me impotent. My enthusiasm fizzles out. Why do I need to gain anything? Isn't it a pleasure just to write? No. Everyone must read, appreciate and congratulate me. It must be published. I must be happy looking at it in print. These are all facts. Why hide them? Why this pretence that I don't have any such hopes?

* * *

Titbits from UG's Childhood

Ever since he was little, UG's independent nature has been so fierce that the consideration of what others might say has disappeared from his dictionary. He always acted according to what he thought was right and never looked for the approval of others or even the approval of the people whom he liked. "Those who know my nature won't think anything [*bad*] about my actions. What do I care about what the people who don't know me think?" he used to argue with his grandmother. UG's logic is, "If there is any truth in what they say [*about me*], I must correct myself; it's useless to be offended by it. If what they say is not true, then there is no need at all to be offended."

* * *

Talking about Bhagavan Ramana Maharshi, UG said, "What did that man in a loin cloth do for me? He did nothing. He made me also a person with a loincloth. That's all." Then he jabs at Ramana: "Why did he keep his mother with him? Why did he build a tomb for her when she died, calling it, *Matrubhuteswara Alayam*? Why did he arrange for worship there? Why did he give traditional answers to the questions of those who came to see him?"

* * *

Malladi Krishnamurti said, "It must be due to our merit from our past lives that has made us not be born as UG's blood relatives. That's our good fortune." That's the comment he made after hearing about all the torment and agony UG had caused his grandmother.

* * *

"You can never know that peace..."

Dr. N. R. R. Rao came from Mysore, along with his wife, on March 8, 1999. UG had just arrived the previous day. Rao was happy to meet UG. "Why is there this misery in us, UG?" Dr. Rao asked. "The body is not interested in anything that you are interested in. That's why there is misery. You are a "squatter" there. The body is throwing you out constantly. All that is put in there by the culture is being thrown out as "oral shit". All that is put in by you as food is thrown out as "anal shit"," said UG.

"From the beginning, the body is throwing you out," UG repeated. "You don't want to leave it gracefully; that's the misery," he added. Dr. Rao again asked, "You say that there is tremendous peace in the organism. How come we are not aware of that peace?"

"You can never know that peace. The body is very peaceful. You are the squatter creating war and violence there," said UG.

* * *

Q: UG, you talk of the "energy" in you. Doesn't that energy flow into us?

UG: Where is the room for it? You're already full. And there is no need to flow at all.

Mohan heard this and started repeating the Upanishadic *mantra* *"purna madah purna midam..."*

* * *

B. S. Shekhawat asked UG, "Why do we come to you?"

UG: You think I have answers to all your questions. But you have the answers. Do you have any questions that nobody has ever asked? All your questions have already been answered. You have the answers. Yet you come and ask for answers.

* * *

"Burn all your maps and break all the compasses. Just drive to reach your destination," said UG once to Paul Sempé.

* * *

Mahesh: UG, why don't you ask me to stop drinking?

UG: You are already in conflict. I don't want to add more to it.

* * *

Q: What is your solution to the problem of poverty in India?

UG: Kill all the Brahmins and wipe out the middle class. That's the only solution.

* * *

Once, Dr. Raghavendra Swami said to UG, "I have decided to drop all pleasure movement from now on, UG."

UG: You will be a dead corpse if you do. Drop it. Don't

announce it. You don't know what will happen afterwards.

* * *

On April 4, 1999, we were at the Farm House. Mahesh called from Bombay. UG answered the phone. Mahesh asked how I was behaving. "He is nasty with me and with Suguna. He is writing nasty things about me," UG complained to him. Mahesh then wanted to talk to me. "Babu, I'm glad you are coming into your own. You finish him with his own ammunition," said Mahesh.

"Not possible, Mahesh, it kills us. It boomerangs."

* * *

"Selectivity and censorship are the only two motives for thinking. There is no thinking if those two are absent," said UG. "'I want', 'I don't want', -- the whole thinking is about that. 'I don't want to think' is also thinking."

* * *

Farm House Discussion

October 19, 1999, Sunday

The eleventh day of the month, Vaikuntha Ekadasi. Vaishnavas believe that today the doors of Vaikuntha [*paradise*] would be wide open and thus on this day they can be certain of being united with Vishnu. Man is not so concerned about how much he should achieve in this life as he is worried about what will happen to him after he dies. How many religions are there in the world and how many faiths! Some believe that they will go to heaven when they die; some that they will be in the proximity of God; others that they will be in the company of Vishnu; and still others that they will have a seat by Jehovah's side. Thus, each culture has its own faith. There are varieties of theories, such as, that there is rebirth after death; that there is no other life; or that only those who are released can be free from rebirth. We have so many discussions, books, lectures, teachings and faiths. Some spend their whole lives concerning themselves with life after death.

Yesterday, Venkata Chalapati, Chandrasekhar, Gopinath, his friend Anil and Majorand I—we all gathered at the Farm House. Chalapati arranged for the meeting at the Farm House unexpectedly and invited me. I accepted. When he and I went on his scooter, the others had already assembled in the *verandah*. We talked about forgetfulness and Alzheimer's disease for a while. Each narrated incidents about his own forgetfulness.

Apparently, Anil came once before to our home to meet UG. He knows me; but I don't remember. I didn't try hard to remember. I can't even remember names let alone faces. Unless I meet them again and again, I don't retain their features in my memory. I can't imagine what they look like. I have always been like that. My memory is weak. That's why my head is no good for gathering information. Recently, I have become even more forgetful. That's why not many things go on in my mind; but what does go on is enough to give me trouble.

Then, the things we discussed yesterday: are enlightened people and gurus on the same level — particularly, four or five people like Sri Ramakrishna Paramahamsa, Bhagawan Ramana Maharshi, UG and J. Krishnamurti? Did J. Krishnamurti drink wine to numb bodily pain? Did Sri Ramakrishna drink *bhang*? Did Bhagawan undergo surgery without anaesthesia? Major said that although UG sneers at these people, probably none of them ever actually used alcohol or drugs. Gopinath claimed that Sri Ramakrishna did not reach the topmost state in his spiritual endeavour. Jiddu did not "pass through" death, he said.

Gopinath thought that UG is in a higher state than all the others; he said that unless a person "passes through" death he is not liberated. My contention is that the actions and words of such an individual do not conform to any known rules. UG contradicts himself and acts contrary to his own assertions. He appears as if he has been working hard to save us from our own imagination and ideas. If we specify that a "free man" acts in such and such a way, then how can we claim that he is completely free? That's why people like UG don't fit into any framework. They are prepared to die at any moment. How could we measure the maturity of such people based on their words and actions? Our measuring rods are false to begin with. Can we use them to measure those who constantly move in the realm of truth? What can we do except stand in their presence with folded hands?

UG incessantly tries to shatter the images that his words create in us. "I am barking like a dog. You create meaning for those sounds and live in the illusion that I am saying something and that you understand it," he says. This too is not real, because you understand it. Such interactions are of no use except to get along in the practical world.

UG's first principle is, "Whatever you think it is, it isn't that," and "To form your own fundamental question," is the first step towards the ultimate state.

Chandrasekhar said that our question must be "How to form a fundamental question?" "Who cares about a fundamental question?" was Gopinath's counter question. That question must formulate itself, I said. It took UG forty-nine years. Our existence must be dissolved in that question. It must grab us; we cannot grab it. Then what should we do? We must always stand in the fixed resolve that nothing can be done. That's all. Not that we must not do anything. We cannot refrain from doing anything. "*Nahi kascit kshanamapi jatu tishthat yakarmakrt*" proclaims the Gita. My head is trying to quote an authority again. That's how it measures. It quotes and shows lines, statements and proofs, and carries on. The gates of the paradise of Vaikuntha are open.

* * *

Valentine's Relatives

December 23, 1999, Thursday — Full Moon Day of the month of Margasira

I returned home from School slightly before noon. Suguna was standing by the gate outside the house. "The Canara Bank manager phoned. Apparently some relatives of Valentine came and have been looking for our address. I gave them directions to our house. They may be here in about ten minutes," she said. I wondered who those relatives could be and fell into a reverie. In a little while, a white Contessa stopped in front of the gate. A young couple about 25 years of age got out of the car. There was another person with them besides the driver. Even with the address it's hard to find our house. I couldn't believe that this foreign couple could find our house without the address, without even knowing our names, but merely by asking around with the help of UG's and Valentine's names.

Apparently, they first enquired in Alliance Françoise; there they only got information about J. Krishnamurti. They were given the vague clue that UG Krishnamurti had lived somewhere near the Tata Silk Farm. They started their search there. Then they went to the Kumaran School in Tata Silk Farm. The Principal there didn't know of Valentine's School. Some people there vaguely knew that

UG Krishnamurti used to live on K.R. Road. So they sent a teacher with them to enquire at Asha Kiran Apartments. They began asking around there. Finally, somebody seems to have suggested that they should enquire at the Canara Bank. They went there and asked about UG and Valentine. After they were given our address there, it took them another couple of hours to get to our house. If they hadn't been able to find us, how disappointed they would have been! They came to Bangalore for just this purpose. Apparently, they have come to Bangalore to see the people who run Valentine's School, to meet and talk with the family who had taken care of Valentine in her final years, and provide any help they can for the School.

Then who are this couple? The young man is the son of Valentine's elder sister Adrienne's daughter; that is, he is Adrienne's grandson. His name is Michael and his wife's name is Agnes. They were married recently. They have come to India on their honeymoon. And they will return to their country on January 6. I can't understand why they have arranged their travel on Gulf Air. When there are so many good airlines, why did they pick Gulf Air? "Because it's cheap," Michael said. He said they will travel by train from Frankfurt to Switzerland.

The couple was pleasant to watch. Apparently, when he was little, his grandmother Adrienne used to tell him stories of Valentine's adventures. Michael related his story: "The first time I saw UG and Valentine together, I was five-years-old. Before every summer, Valentine used to spend a few days with her sisters. The first few times UG accompanied her. Then only Valentine went and stayed in Lugano and Moulouse for a month each summer. It was UG who encouraged Valentine to spend some time each year with her two sisters. By herself, she was reluctant to have relationships with members of her family.

Michael also knew of the merging of Valentine's ashes in Kaveri Sangamam after her death. Apparently his grandmother or mother appreciated the act very much. It's their custom to bury all the dead members of a family in the same place. "But Valentine had a peculiar personality. She separated herself from the family early in her life and lived a life of adventure. It's appropriate that the remains of such a lady also got merged in a river, contrary to her tradition," Michael's grandmother had said, according to Michael. He expressed his wish to see that place. I told the driver to stop the car on the Western Bank of the river on their way to Mysore and show them the stream of the river. Last evening around 6 p.m., they both left for Mysore.

* * *

The six hours they spent with us passed like six minutes while we dug up our memories of Valentine and talking about her, watching videos and looking at photos. Michael and Agnes knew that we are running Valentine School. But the weather yesterday was terrible. Ever since the morning, the sky was overcast and by the afternoon the sky became cloudy and it rained. It was cold and messy. Yet we went there, and they learned all the information about Valentine very patiently and looked at everything with great interest. They took pictures of each and every classroom in the school. They saw the album of photos of the fancy dress competition. They watched the video on Valentine, the video album of their family. They said they would definitely give help to the School.

Their coming and seeing the school, discussing everything, thanking me and Suguna wholeheartedly for taking care of Valentine in her last days, their mingling with us nicely, dining with us, enquiring about UG and his philosophy, learning about it and discussing it with us—all these delighted us very much. Michael gave me two thousand rupees saying, "Please take this as our donation for the present."

* * *

Valentine's sister Rose has a daughter called Maria. She married a much older man who was her violin teacher; he was totally blind. He is dead now and she lives in Paris. Michael and Agnes live in Neuchâtel, Switzerland. Valentine had an adventurous spirit. Michael told us that many in the de Kerven family had that trait of adventurousness. One of the ancestors in the de Kerven family apparently surveyed the whole of Greenland. A mountain in

Greenland is named after him. Another ancestor, a lady, was also adventurous like Valentine. She became renowned for riding on a horse from Argentina in South America to Washington, DC.

Michael had heard, even as a child, of Valentine's crossing the Sahara Desert on a motorcycle. Agnes is still surprised that he mentioned that incident when he first met Agnes in a hotel. Both, Agnes and I both appreciated his love and affection for Valentine. Suguna and I were pleased that after so many years, some relatives of Valentine, although they are not her own immediate family, travelled such a great distance to come here, eat with us and talk to us about everything. I don't know to what extent they will provide help to the School, the School that remains as a memorial to Valentine, but it's amazing that they came all this distance and showed interest in meeting us.

A Prayer to UG

December 29, 1999, Wednesday

UG's harangues have started again. He has sent me a copy of his e-mail to Bob. Besides criticising India, he complains in the letter that my behaviour and I are extraordinary and are preventing him from coming to India and that I am tormenting Suguna.

I know my behaviour and my mind very well. My mind has been struggling to move away from UG and step out of UG's way as much as possible. Nowadays, I am not relishing anything connected with UG. I don't feel like listening to UG's tapes. I don't feel like talking about him. I don't feel like listening to what he says. I don't feel like seeing him, spending time with him or inviting him to India. When I hear that he is coming to India, trains run in my heart! I worry, thinking, "Why in the world is he coming?" I have been going around picking up things to do as if they are the most important things in the world and not bothering about UG's affairs at all. Moreover, I have been reconciling myself by telling myself, "UG has turned me into such a person through his behaviour." I have been justifying my behaviour by telling myself that it's only due to his constant efforts to keep me away that this desire to move away from him has taken root in me. When I read that e-mail yesterday, my mind has become troubled.

After I went with Suguna to the hospital and the doctors described Raghavendra Rao's condition to us and told us that it's impossible for him to live, or rather to keep him alive, my mind cowered even more. Some unknown fears came rushing! Although I was reassuring Aruna and Venkat and offering them words of advice, I was agitated. What's going to happen? What things are going to end at the end of the year, at the end of the millennium? I hear the sound of someone roaring, "This is not the end; this is the beginning!"

I know why UG has been ranting and raving about me. Although it's clear to me that he knows what's happening in my heart of hearts, my mind wouldn't admit it. My tricky mind uses ploys to find fault with UG and say, "You are the cause of all this misfortune; all this is happening because of you." UG instantly knows all my thoughts, plans and ploys. I am also aware that he knows instantly that my mind is striving constantly to become distant from him and to escape from my life as it relates to him, and that it is trying to forget itself in vain through these various meaningless activities.

This is not a game. UG is none other than Siva incarnate. There are no boundaries there. Although all that happens in my head is not reflected there, UG vibrates in accordance with them. No matter how he vibrates, his vibrations reflect my behaviour and personality. I can't control the turmoil generated by my mind. "What should I do now?" "What could I do that would please UG?" "What sort of behaviour would please UG?" — it's useless to think in these lines. The real "I" in myself, the "I" which nested itself in me and the "I" which arrogates to itself constantly that "I am doing it" — that "I" is the real problem. UG's message is not a divine symbol; it's a direct command. UG knows all my attempts to prolong this separation, to escape from him by staying away, to hide behind walls and backs and steal away like a thief and avoid being detected. As soon as I think "Finally, it's safe here, let me rest," the ubiquitous UG taps on my shoulder. Where can I escape? I say, "*Anyatha saranam nasti, tvameva saranam mama,*" [*You are my only refuge; I have no other rescue.*] and I plot to escape by taking refuge.

"A sanskrit verse adapted from the 'Venkateswara

Suprabhatam'[Good morning to Lord Venkateswara] is ringing in my ears and runs on my lips. *Ajnanina maya dosha nyaseshan vihitan Sive! Kshamasvathvam Kshamasvatvam Sri UG Paramathmane!* I am reciting to myself. "I have committed many wrongs in my ignorance, O The Soul Divine! UG! Please forgive me. Be merciful to me. Don't burn me like this. Don't let me desire anything but you. Even by tormenting me, cleansing me or tearing me into pieces, hold me within you. This life of mine is granted by you. It must be completely dedicated to you. Please make sure that it's not wasted. Everything is in your hands. Save me from the evil thoughts of rejecting you and moving away from your presence, and turn me towards you. Please listen to my prayer at least at the end of this millennium. You can burn me, torture me or torment me; but save me from this goblet of poison. This is my prayer, Lord," I feel like blurting out before UG's photograph.

In Conclusion...

"I want to die unknown, unwept, unsung and un-honoured. But, when I said this to Moorty, he remarked, 'UG! This will not happen as long as Chandrasekhar is near you at the time of your death. He will never allow this kind of a thing to happen,'" said UG, looking at me half mockingly and half jokingly with a bemused smile. The next moment the room full of people burst forth into loud laughter. I had witnessed this scene almost a dozen times that year ever since UG arrived in Bangalore on February 14, 2006.

That day when UG repeated the same line and looked at me intently, I was seized by a sudden unknown impulse. I moved towards him, sat at his feet and said in a serious tone, "UG! I don't want to be around you when you die. Please see that I am nowhere near you. Or pack me up from this world before you go. That solves the problem." UG smiled and said in a low tone, "Packing you up is not going to happen... I can't wait that long..." I felt relieved that I had said my piece and totally forgot about it later. But little did I imagine that UG used this request to keep me away from him when he chose to exit from this world. Exactly a year later, on March 14, 2007, in Vallecrosia when UG asked Suguna and me also to leave and go back to Bangalore, it suddenly dawned on me that UG was really determined to quit this world. He was fulfilling the request

I made a year ago.

Many astrologers had predicted earlier that UG was blessed with the power of "shedding the body at will," which they term as Ichha Maranayoga. UG lived all his life on his own terms and when he felt that the time had come to quit the world, he orchestrated his own death and died on his own terms.

It all started on January 31, 2007 after he had a fall in Vallecrosia, Italy. On the night of February 9, he called me and said, "Chandrasekhar! My travels have come to an end. I am not coming to India as planned. I am not going to America. My idea is to go to Gstaad after I get better. If you both want to bid me 'Final Good-bye', come to Vallecrosia. Come with Mahesh." He insisted that we get the Swiss visa too, so that we could go with him to Gstaad. We were startled at first, then immediately began making our travel plans to reach UG as early as possible.

In the meantime, many friends from all parts of the world started converging in Vallecrosia. By then, Moorty was ready with the translations of my books "Stopped in our tracks — Series II" and "Series III" and managed to reach Vallecrosia by February 15. In spite of his deteriorating physical condition, UG evinced keen interest in the contents of these two books. The books were going around and friends were reading out parts of them to UG. Apparently, Guha had read the chapter Kathopanishad to UG. Much later, Moorty wrote to me that UG had exclaimed just after listening to it, "What a good scholar Chandrasekhar is!" I was overjoyed. The greatest thing that happened to me was Moorty reading out the last chapter "A Prayer to UG" to UG. Lisa videotaped the entire event. My Lord had heard what I wanted to convey to him. What more could I want? After both of us [Suguna and I] got there, UG asked me to read some pages from my book "Stopped in our tracks —Series III".

In my first book I had written, "This story has no head or tail." Yes. It has no beginning and no end. How can anybody end such a story? It has to go on like the day and the night: one following the other. I cannot but recall what UG often said, "What I say doesn't need the support of any kind. If there is anything to it, it will stand all by itself. My words have their own authority."

True UG! Your words do not need any support. On the other hand, I need their support for my existence. For my continuation. It is always my need. My need. My need indeed!

***

A scene in Bangalore 2006

Brhamachari, Chandrasekhar, UG and Moorty

A Scene in Farmhouse-2004

Actress Sridevi with UG in Hongkong

Aruna, UG, Archana and Aparajita

Jitendra Baba with UG-Bangalore

Mahesh & Chandrasekhar

Chandrasekhar, UG & Shekhawat

Vedam Satyanarayana and UG

Valentine's family in Bangalore with UG

A scene in Bangalore-1981

UG and Chandrasekhar in the farm house

Sharmila & Bharati with UG-2002

UG in 1994

U.G. KRISHNAMURTI'S BIRTH CHART
(NIRAYANA SYSTEM)

DATE OF BIRTH : JULY 9, 1918
TIME : 06.12:32" AM (IST)
PLACE OF BIRTH : MASULIPATAM
BIRTH STAR : PUNARVASU 4 PADAM
LAGNAM : MITHUNA LAGNAM – 29° 30'
BALANCE DASA AT THE TIME OF BIRTH : GURU DASA – 1y – 10m – 17d

RASI

	SUKRA / KETU	RAVI PLUTO-12°22' / GURU NEP 13°14' / SANI BUDHA CHANDRA	RAHU
URANUS 4°40'			
			SANI
	RAHU	KUJA	

AMSA

		RAVI KUJA	SUKRA
			CHANDRA
	GURU		BUDHA KETU

PLANETS	SIGN POSITION	DEGREE POSITION	STAR POSITION	STAR LORD
RAVI	MITHUNA	23° 24'	PUNARVASU 2	GURU
CHANDRA	KATAKA	1° 46'	PUNARVASU 4	GURU
KUJA	KANYA	14° 53'	HASTA 2	CHANDRA
BUDHA	KATAKA	6° 47'	PUSHYA 2	SANI
GURU	MITHUNA	6° 27'	MRIGASIRA 3	KUJA
SUKRA	VRISHABHA	18° 45'	ROHINI 3	CHANDRA
SANI	KATAKA	21° 11'	ASLESHA 2	BUDHA
RAHU	VRISCHIKA	28° 24'	JYESHTA 4	BUDHA
KETU	VRISHABHA	28°	MRIGASIRA 2	KUJA

UG's Birth Chart with Planetary positions
Nirayana System